KRISTEN TIBER

a HEART for Journey

Developing Purpose, Faith,
and a Biblical Mindset
for the Road of Life

Copyright © 2023
All Rights Reserved
Kristen Tiber | Kristen Summers LLC

No part of this publication may be reproduced, distributed, or transmitted in any form or by any means, including photocopying, recording, or other electronic or mechanical methods, without the prior written permission of the publisher, except in the case of brief quotations embodied in reviews and certain other non-commercial uses permitted by copyright law.

All Scripture quotations, unless otherwise indicated, are taken from the Holy Bible, New International Version®, NIV®. Copyright ©1973, 1978, 1984, 2011 by Biblica, Inc.™ Used by permission of Zondervan. All rights reserved worldwide. www.zondervan.com. The "NIV" and "New International Version" are trademarks registered in the United States Patent and Trademark Office by Biblica, Inc.™

All Scriptures noted with NKJV are taken from the New King James Version®. Copyright © 1982 by Thomas Nelson. Used by permission. All rights reserved.

All Scriptures noted with ESV are from The ESV® Bible (The Holy Bible, English Standard Version®), copyright © 2001 by Crossway, a publishing ministry of Good News Publishers. Used by permission. All rights reserved.

All Scriptures noted with NIV 1984 are taken from the HOLY BIBLE, NEW INTERNATIONAL VERSION®. Copyright © 1973, 1978, 1984 by International Bible Society. Used by permission of Zondervan Publishing House. All rights reserved.

ISBN: 978–0–9995876–2-1 (paperback), 978–0–9995876–3-8 (epub)

Publishing and Design Services: MelindaMartin.me

www.KristenTiber.com

For Dan,
always pushing me beyond
my *destination* mindset
and encouraging me
to enjoy the *journey*.

Contents

	Introduction 1
Week One	Road Ready 3
Week Two	A Return Trip 31
Week Three	Together 59
Week Four	A Heart to Serve 87
Week Five	The Road Ahead 117

About the Author 145

How to Have a Personal Relationship with Jesus 147

Leader's Guide 150

Acknowledgements 153

Works Cited 155

Introduction

A few summers ago, I was writing for a ferry company that carries guests to and from the islands of Put-In-Bay in Lake Erie. The company provided our passage to the island and gave us a golf cart to drive around South Bass Island.

I will tell you, it was very weird for the first several hours driving this golf cart down real roads with real cars. But this wasn't just any golf cart you'd find on an 18-hole course. This golf cart was "road-ready," which meant it had turn signals and lights, and it could go faster than those driven by recreational golfers. This cart was prepared and ready for actual roads and not just the picturesque paths between the tees and the greens.

On this journey of life, what do we need in order to be "road-ready"? Over the next five weeks, we are going to dig into the Scriptures and look at what it means to have a heart for the journey the Lord wants to take us on. We will discover that the Lord is interested not only in our eternal destination (which is of utmost importance), but that He also cares about our journeys here and now.

We will look at what it means to be journeying with God in a world and culture that are very challenging and antagonistic to the things of God. Where do we need to focus, what is our purpose, and what are our priorities? What does a biblical perspective look like? Do we need other people or can we just go it alone? Where do we find hope and strength, and how do we get through this life without being ripped apart when we look at everything around us? We will work to answer these questions and more through the pages of the Word and the lives of fellow pilgrims found within.

Are you ready? Let's hit the road and get started!

How to Get the Most Out of This Study

This workbook is accompanied by online teaching videos. You'll start first with the introduction video which can be found at www.KristenTiber.com/AHeartForJourneyVideos. An email address will be required to access the videos, and you'll receive immediate access to a special link just for you. After you watch the introduction video, you'll be ready and I hope excited to dive into this study.

After you complete each week in the workbook, watch the corresponding week's video. You will find a page at the end of each week in your workbook on which to take notes. There are five weeks of workbook lessons and six videos (including the introduction video).

If you are doing this with a group, you will find a Leader's Guide in the back of this workbook. Questions marked with ✢ are intended for group discussion.

As you read the Scripture passages and complete the questions in the workbook each week, I am praying that the Lord gives you a heart for journey and mightily increases your faith and trust in the One who loves you so much and is with you always.

For His Glory,

Week One

Road-Ready

"Blessed be the God and Father of our Lord Jesus Christ, who has blessed us in Christ with every spiritual blessing in the heavenly places, even as he chose us in him before the foundation of the world, that we should be holy and blameless before him. In love he predestined us for adoption to himself as sons through Jesus Christ, according to the purpose of his will, to the praise of his glorious grace, with which he has blessed us in the Beloved."

EPHESIANS 1:3–6 ESV

Day One

Welcome! Today, we begin our adventure through the Scriptures as we work to develop our own heart for journey. There are many great examples of journeys in the Bible at which we could look. So many sojourners and fellow pilgrims.

�֍When you think of journeys in the Bible, what comes to mind?

I think of Abraham leaving Haran and following God to a new land. I think of Jacob returning to his homeland and encountering the Lord in a wrestling match on the way. What about Moses and the Israelites' departure out of Egypt and their crossing of the Red Sea? Or their forty years in the desert until the time came when they were able to enter the Promised Land? I remember the Israelites journeying to Jerusalem for the three annual festivals. I think of Jonah, Daniel, Shadrach, Meshach, Abednego, Ezra, Nehemiah, and the exiles in Babylon returning to Jerusalem.

New Testament journeys bring to mind Mary and Joseph traveling to Bethlehem and Egypt, Jesus and His disciples trekking around Israel, and Saul on the road to Damascus. I think of the travels of the early church, the missionary journeys of Paul, and even the diaspora—those believers who journeyed to far off places in order to avoid persecution. This resulted in the spreading of the Gospel like seed scattered in the field of the world.

Throughout this study, we will be looking at different journeys in the Bible. We will discover the characteristics and traits that marked those who possessed a heart for going the distance with God, in order that we too might develop a heart for the journey the Lord wants to take *us* on.

Week One

Let's start our study by exploring Psalm 84 more thoroughly. As I shared in the introduction video (please go back and watch it online if you missed it), this life is a journey. It is a highway with different stops along the way. And how we view this journey can make a difference between a joy-filled life and a lack-luster experience, between a purpose-driven path and an empty existence. What would you like to mark your journey? What kind of trip do you want it to be?

Fill in the blanks below:

"Blessed are those whose _____ is in you, whose _____ are set on _____." Psalm 84:5

What do you think this means? What does it mean to have a heart for pilgrimage?

Throughout this week, I'd love for you to work on memorizing this verse. Why not start by writing Psalm 84:5 on a notecard and putting it in a conspicuous spot?

Now let's take a step back in order to discover the context of the whole psalm. What is at play here? Read Psalm 84 (including the introduction) and write down any observations.

Scholars differ on whom they believe wrote this psalm. Some think it was written by David for the sons of Korah to put to music. Others think it was the sons of Korah who penned the psalm, directing attention to the common themes (like Zion) that often pervade their other songs. I lean toward the sons' authorship, but either way, one thing is certain: the sons of Korah are definitely connected with Psalm 84. But who were these men? What place did they have in tabernacle worship? And who is Korah? Let's go back several hundreds of years to discover the answers. Ready for the trip?

Read Numbers 16:1–11. What did Korah do?

Read Numbers 16:25–35. What happened to Korah and his followers?

According to Numbers 26:9–11, did the line of Korah die out? _____

Korah was the first cousin of Moses and Aaron (Exod. 6:21), but he was not a righteous person. He was rebellious and prideful. Not only did Korah accuse Moses of putting himself above the community, but he also tried to promote his own position (16:10), ultimately rebelling against the Lord Himself. And what was the consequence for such insolence? We saw that the Lord caused the earth to swallow up Korah and the others, followed by fire that consumed the 250 men who had joined them.

What a sight that must have been! Imagine going back into your tents after witnessing such a graphic scene. And yet, the hearts of the people remained hard, and the whole community continued to grumble the next day against Moses and Aaron. So the Lord brought a plague against the people that only stopped after Aaron made atonement for their sin. But even so, the name of Korah had been soiled and stained, and the mark would not soon be forgotten.

However, the sons of Korah did not stand ruined by their association with their ancestor. While Korah was known for rebellion, his descendants were known for worship. In all, there are eleven beautiful psalms attributed to the sons of Korah. The sons were put in charge of the music after the ark came to rest in the tabernacle until Solomon built the temple in Jerusalem (1 Chron. 6:31–37). This Levitical family served God in many ways,[1] including as gatekeepers at the temple (1 Chron. 9:19). God redeemed their lineage!

Among some of their most well-known lyrics are verses like "God is our refuge and strength, an ever-present help in trouble. Therefore we will not fear, though the earth give way and the mountains fall into the heart of the sea, though its waters roar and foam and the mountains quake with their surging" (Ps. 46:1–3).

In light of their relative's dramatic demise, do you see any irony in these words from Psalm 46? What did you notice?

Why is all this worth knowing? You see, the sons' journey was not defined by their ancestor. And likewise, your journey through this life is not defined by those who came before you. It does not matter where you come from, what your background is, your level of education, how much money is in your bank account, who your parents are, nor what they did. God is bigger than all of that.

What do you think defines your journey? What have you allowed to define it?

Is it a label you were given long ago? Is it an event or a rough past? None of these things define you. You are defined by One. And He is the giver of life, the redeemer of souls, the forgiver of sin, and the restorer of lives. You are the apple of His eye and the object of His affection. Nothing else needs to define your journey.

Let me add that if your walk has been defined by a sinful past, the Lord can put you on a new path. Sure, repentance for sin is still necessary. We need to confess, repent, and turn away. But that does not need to characterize your journey from here on out. God will use what lies behind in your past, but it does not determine your future.

Because when we are in Christ, we are a new creation (2 Cor. 5:17). He takes the old and makes it new. The Lord can take what was unstable, shoddy, and messy and put your feet on solid ground—new dirt and all. I know people who have all sorts of different things in their past—things that would surprise many people—but in Christ, God has provided a new direction. It is beautiful. It is redemption.

Just as the descendants of Korah were redeemed from their grievous lineage, we as believers in Jesus have been redeemed from the penalty of sin and death. We are given new life. (If you do not know what it means to be saved or to be in a relationship with Jesus, please turn to page 147 to learn more.)

The path before you can be an incredible journey. But this is not your parents' paths, your husband's path, your children's paths, or your best friend's path. This is *your* path. This is your journey with God. Yes, your path will connect with others (and we will talk about that later), but how you approach your journey is all on you. You can be single-minded with focus on the destination alone, or you can have eyes set on the open road of possibilities of what God wants to do in you and through you. You are the one who needs a heart for journey. And my friend, blessings await.

"He lifted me out of the slimy pit, out of the mud and mire; he set my feet on a rock and gave me a firm place to stand."

—PSALM 40:2

"So I will restore to you the years that the swarming locust has eaten."

—JOEL 2:25 NKJV

Read more about what it means to have a relationship with Christ on page 147.

Is this good news? What does this mean to you?

✢ **What are you hoping for during these next five weeks as we look at developing a heart for journey?**

Now that we have the context for this psalm under our belts, tomorrow we'll jump into the content and discover what stirred the hearts and minds of the sons of Korah. Get ready! We're going to Jerusalem.

> What is one of our goals on this journey? To bring glory to God with our whole lives.

Day Two

Now that the dust has settled on the ground above Korah, let's turn from who his descendants were, to what the sons of Korah wrote as we work our way toward verse five, our theme verse for the study. Psalm 84 has often been characterized as a "pilgrim song."[2] What journey was the pilgrim psalmist going on? Let's take a look.

> ✢ **Please read Psalm 84:1–2 again. What things drew the psalmist's affection and desire?**

It is thought that the psalmist was either finally returning to Jerusalem after having been prevented from going (for whatever reason) or that he was on a pilgrimage to Jerusalem for one of the three annual feasts that brought people to the city. Either scenario works. And even though this particular psalm is sandwiched in what's called Book Three of the Psalms (Pss. 73–89)—a group of psalms that primarily deal with communal or national issues[3]—you'll notice that Psalm 84 is incredibly individualistic. The psalmist was speaking personally with deep desire and conviction. Can you sense his passion? These are the feelings of someone who desired to be near God and His dwelling place.

When have you felt this passionate over something?

When I was a young teen, I was passionate about dolphins. I wanted to work with dolphins; I wanted to save the dolphins. I had dolphin this and dolphin that. And this lasted for a couple of years. But eventually the strong interest came to an end. When my son, Peter, was very young, he was consumed with trains. He watched train videos. He played with Thomas, Chuggington, and Geo Trax sets. He even named his trains after people he liked. We had Little Janet, Little Aunt Lynn, Train Grandma, and more. The kid lived, breathed *and talked* trains all the time. It was his focus. It was his obsession for several years, but then it too came to an end. The psalmist, however, wasn't dealing with some kind of passing fad or interest. He longed not only for God's courts and dwelling place, but he also desired to be near the Most High Himself.

And for the psalmist, being near the Lord was a reality. As much as I loved dolphins during those teen years, I wasn't able to be near the real thing. Oh how I longed to swim and play with dolphins in the ocean, but there was a problem. I lived in Ohio! We have a beautiful Great Lake near us, but let's be real, there are no dolphins here. There was zero chance of me being near an actual dolphin other than watching the twenty-minute dolphin show at Sea World Ohio (before it closed).

The psalmist, on the other hand, ministered at the tabernacle and had experienced the real thing. He had tasted and seen that the Lord is good (Ps. 34:8). He knew the might and power of the Lord. In fact, let's look at what the psalmist called God.

Write down all the names or titles the psalmist used for God in Psalm 84:1–4.

We are going to look at two in particular. Depending on which Bible version you are using, the first name you see is LORD Almighty or LORD of Hosts. Unfortunately, the NIV translates two different Hebrew names for God into the one English name, LORD Almighty. However, LORD of Hosts is the better translation here. In Hebrew, the name is *Yahweh Sabaoth*, and it signifies the leader of an army, a heavenly army. Our God is over all the angelic creatures as well as the whole earth. This is a name that is powerful, mighty, and strong. And this is the name specifically used first by the writer.

✣How do you see God? If you had to write a name for Him, what would it be? What would it reflect?

The other description we will look at is living God. This title for God only appears in one other place in the Psalms.

Read Psalm 42:1–2 in the margin. Do you see parallel desires in this psalm and in Psalm 84? What imagery is used here?

"As the deer pants for streams of water, so my soul pants for you, my God. My soul thirsts for God, for the living God. When can I go and meet with my God?"

—PSALM 42:1–2

Here again, we see the writer's deep desire to be with God, the *living* God. The sons of Korah knew God was alive and real. They knew it personally. And oh, how it affected and transformed their lives into this great desire for His presence.

We worship a living God. But not all did. For contrast, please read Psalm 115:1–8. How are the man-made idols described?

Is there any comparison between the Hebrew God and the idols or gods of that day? No, there is not. The Hebrew God was and is alive. The others were not, nor will they ever be. How does this thought carry through to our day? Our idols may not be carved out of stone or wood, but we certainly have idols in our culture today—things that we worship intentionally or unintentionally.

> *"All who make idols are nothing, and the things they treasure are worthless."*
>
> —ISAIAH 44:9A

Name some of our culture's idols.

Do you give any idol a place in your life?

When you compare these idols and their eternal significance to the one true and living God, what is your conclusion?

Our God is living. He moves. He hears. He changes hearts and lives. He is still in the business of the miraculous. He has a long history of incredible deeds. And about two thousand years ago, He put His feet on the ground of Earth because of His love for us. He set aside His glory so that He Himself could be the atoning sacrifice (1 John 2:2). He was crucified and paid the hefty price that we owed for our sin. But He didn't stay dead. He rose from the grave and lives today. And what does all this cost us? Nothing. It is free. He did this out of love—out of His great love for you.

> *"I am the Living One; I was dead, and now look, I am alive for ever and ever! And I hold the keys of death and Hades."*
>
> —REVELATION 1:18

Does that make you long for His presence? When I consider who He is and what He has done, I want to draw near, to love Him with my whole heart, and to be found in His presence. The psalmist wanted simply to be near Him. But what strikes me most right now is that as much as you may want to be near Him, the living God wants even more to be near you. His love for you is that spectacular! He is not just a distant God who spun the world into being and stepped back. He desires to be intimately involved in our lives, in our journeys. Isn't that amazing? I'm in awe.

You see, one of the most important things we can have on our journey through this life is a passion and hunger for God. And I understand that our desire can wax and wane at times. But as soon as you sense it is diminishing, halt! Slam on the brakes. Stop and yield. Join the sons of Korah, and make time with Him your foremost passion and priority.

Do you share the psalmist's desire? Do you want this passion? Write a prayer asking the living God to increase your hunger for Him.

> "Then you will call on me and come and pray to me, and I will listen to you. You will seek me and find me when you seek me with all your heart."
>
> —JEREMIAH 29:12–13

> "Draw near to God and he will draw near to you."
>
> —JAMES 4:8A ESV

> A heart for journey is marked by a passion for God and His presence.

Day Three

I am so thankful for GPSs, aren't you? How often I would have been lost or on the wrong path without the instruction, "In 500 feet, turn left." And while I dread the "Make a U-turn," I am still thankful for consistent and good instruction when I choose to follow what it says.

In yesterday's lesson, we talked about having a passion for God and His presence that transforms our lives. It characterizes what we focus on and seek after. Today, we're going to venture away from Psalm 84 just long enough to look at what happens when we aren't hungering after and seeking God. As we will quickly see, the lack of this passion leads down the wrong road. And Israel and her kings weren't quick with U-turns!

A Heart for Journey

Fill in the blanks about Rehoboam, the son of Solomon, based on 2 Chronicles 12:14.

"He did _____ because he had not set his _____ on _____ the LORD."

Rehoboam was not only the son of King Solomon, but he was also his successor—well, at least for a while. Because of poor decisions and heeding foolish counsel, Rehoboam was the last king of Israel's unified monarchy. Under his rule, the kingdom split into the northern kingdom of Israel and the southern kingdom of Judah. While the north had not been pleased with Solomon's taxation and harsh labor,[4] it was Rehoboam's poor handling of these issues that ultimately provoked the northern tribes to secede (1 Kings 12). Rehoboam then became the first king of Judah, the southern kingdom.

Under Rehoboam's rule, Judah set up "high places, sacred stones and Asherah poles on every high hill and under every spreading tree. There were even male shrine prostitutes in the land; the people engaged in all the detestable practices of the nations the LORD had driven out before the Israelites" (1 Kings 14:23–24). No, Rehoboam was not seeking God in his reign and rule. He was going his own way, down his own path—and apparently, leading an entire kingdom in that direction as well.

What happens when we fail to seek God? When we neglect to seek God—whether individually, as a family, or as a church—everything gets off track. Or should I say off the good path? And the northern kingdom of Israel wasn't in much better shape.

Let's jump forward in time to the years of the prophet Amos. Turn to Amos 5:4–6. What did God instruct His people to do?

✤ What did He tell them *not* to do? Be specific.

While Rehoboam was the first king of Judah, Jeroboam I became the first king of the northern kingdom, Israel. And by the time Amos became a prophet, Israel was fourteen kings down the royal line with Jeroboam II at the helm. (It would seem like Jeroboam II should immediately follow the first, but it doesn't always work that way.)

Jeroboam I was the first king of Israel and Jeroboam II was the fourteenth. The years between the two monarchs spelled out a rollercoaster of good and bad leadership for both the northern and southern kingdoms. Good kings were rare and bad kings were prevalent. Amos entered the scene when Jeroboam II was reigning over Israel. The people had embraced Baal worship and fertility cults.[5] And so God called Amos to prophesy against Israel. Scary, right? I can't help but wonder how Amos felt. He was not a prophet by profession or lineage; he was a shepherd and a farmer (Amos 7:14–15). Telling sheep they've gone astray is very different than rebuking human beings.

Look again at what Amos told the people of Israel. He told them to seek God and live. He said not to seek Bethel, not to go to Gilgal, nor to journey to Beersheba. One important thing to know about all three of these locations was that at one time, they were very special places with great significance.

We first hear of Bethel when Abraham pitched his tent nearby and built an altar to the Lord (Gen. 12 and 13). It was in Bethel that Jacob received the vision of the staircase to heaven with the angels ascending and descending. Jacob named this site Bethel, which means "house of God" (Gen. 28). Throughout the years that followed, Bethel was a place of worship. For a time, it was the location of the ark of the covenant (Judg. 20), and where the Israelites would go to inquire of the Lord during times of trouble.

Gilgal was the first campsite of the Israelites after they crossed the Jordan and entered the Promised Land. This was the place where each tribe pulled a

> *"I was neither a prophet nor the son of a prophet, but I was a shepherd, and I also took care of sycamore-fig trees. But the LORD took me from tending the flock and said to me, 'Go, prophesy to my people Israel.'"*
>
> —AMOS 7:14–15

stone out of the Jordan River, and Joshua built the stones into a memorial as a remembrance so that when their children asked what the stones meant, they would hear the great account of what God had done (Josh. 4). Gilgal was the staging grounds for Joshua before he led the people against Jericho and the site of the first Passover in Canaan (Josh. 5). King Saul's coronation took place in Gilgal (1 Sam. 11), and this was where the people gathered to welcome David back as king after his son's revolt (2 Sam. 19).[6]

Beersheba, at the southern part of the Promised Land (eventually the southern kingdom), was the place where Abraham made an oath with Abimelech, where God appeared to Hagar in the wilderness, and where Abraham dug a well and planted a tamarisk tree (Gen. 21). God also appeared to Isaac and Jacob at Beersheba (Gen. 26 and 46, respectively).

These places were rich with history and remembrances of God's faithfulness. But they didn't stay that way. Bethel became one of two sites that housed golden calves for the people to worship in the northern kingdom. It became a city teeming with idolatry, condemned by Jeremiah, Amos, and Hosea. Hosea even called it Beth Aven which means "house of idols." Gilgal also became a city of idolatry condemned by the prophets, and Beersheba deteriorated into a place of pilgrimage for idol worship.

In Amos 5, God warned His people not to chase after these places, not to journey for idol worship, nor run after things that are false, but to seek Him, the true and living God so that they may live. Judgement was coming, but the Lord still gave the people an invitation to change their ways. In the end however, they did not. Bethel and Gilgal were taken into captivity very soon after this time, and Beersheba in the southern kingdom followed a similar fate over a hundred years later.

✢ **Can you think of a time when you chased after the wrong things? What was the outcome?**

Why is it important to seek God?

You see, the path we take is important. Seeking God for the journey is vital. God not only takes our destination seriously, but He also values our journey. There will be many roads you can take in this life, but consistently seeking God helps us stay on the right path. To do otherwise leads down a dangerous road.

So then, how do we seek Him? How do we identify the right path? A primary way we discover what is good and right is by studying His Word, the Bible. Reading, studying, and knowing His Word will be a light to our path, at all times and in all ways. And that is what we're doing right here!

A heart for journey seeks after God and His ways.

In fact, let's look up that verse. What does Psalm 119:105 tell us that the Word of God is?

The Bible is alive and active (Heb. 4:12). And it is exciting! In it, we have everything we need for this life. Read 2 Timothy 3:16–17 in the margin and underline how Scripture helps us.

"All Scripture is God-breathed and is useful for teaching, rebuking, correcting and training in righteousness, so that the servant of God may be thoroughly equipped for every good work."

—2 TIMOTHY 3:16–17

There are lots of places we can go to for advice, but not all of them will be biblical. We have to know the Word in order to sift through those who convey biblical truth and those who push the concept of personal truth. Plant yourself in the Word. Abide in the Word. This is how we will know the path that God has for us.

Recently, I was reading through a journal entry I had made when the kids were small and found this: "Anna (one year old) is a total copycat to whatever her big brother Peter does. One night, Peter went over and bopped his six-month-old cousin Lucy on the head. Anna stopped what she was doing, stood up, walked over, and bopped that sweet child on the head as well."

Whose path was Anna on? Certainly not the one that says love your neighbor, and do good to others. Now, can I fault a very young child for copying? No. But I was able to teach her and her bold, older brother what was right. We can't be walking in the steps of others unless we know they align with the Word of God. There are some very loud voices out there these days and our ears need to be alert to the occasions when the suggested path does not line up with Scripture.

Simply put, we have to watch who we follow and what we chase after. But diligently seeking God and knowing the Word will keep us in line every time. Rehoboam and many of the kings didn't seek after God. Their path led to destruction. What road are you on? Do you need to change lanes or even make a U-turn?

�֍**What can you do to be more deliberate about seeking God?**

We'll be back in Psalm 84 and digging into our theme verse tomorrow. See you then!

Day Four

Today, we get back to our theme verse in Psalm 84:5. Have you started memorizing it? Write it out below and then circle the key words.

What did you circle? I circled the words *blessed, strength, heart,* and *pilgrimage.* The Hebrew word for blessed is the word *esher,* and it speaks to happiness and blessedness.[7] Happy are those who do what? This verse tells us there are two things. First, happy are those who find their strength in God, the living God.

When you go through something challenging, do you operate in your own strength or in God's? Do you press in and rely on Him for endurance, peace, wisdom, and perseverance? Or do you rely upon yourself? I know my tendencies, but I also know it doesn't work when I rely on my own stubborn strength. God's strength is all-sufficient for your journey and my friend, it has no limits.

The year after we built our house, we put in the lawn. Boy, who would have thought rock-hogging, landscaping, and grass seed could cost so much? I am so glad my builder warned me in advance to set aside some money for that.

The week that the lawn was seeded, Dan was heading out of town for work, which left the task of watering the newly seeded ground to me. We have a very big front yard, and because you aren't supposed to walk very much on freshly seeded or sprouting grass, we had set up multiple sprinklers in various places to water as efficiently as we could and minimize how much we trekked on the ground.

One evening before dusk, I went out to turn on the hoses and move the sprinklers somewhat as I started the nightly ritual. I ran two of the sprinklers as usual, but then in an attempt to move things along more quickly, I decided to turn on a third one as well.

In theory, it was a good idea. But when I went outside a couple of hours later to check, I found that *everything* had stopped. There wasn't any stream of water flicking across the grass. I put a nozzle on one hose to try to figure out what the problem was, hoping it was a sprinkler issue. Then a thought of horror crossed my mind.

Could I have run our well dry? We had only been living in the house for a year. The well was only one year old! Could I have dried up the well? And if so, what damage did I just cause?

Enter the sick feeling in my stomach.

Since Dan was out of town and unable to be reached, I called his cousin (a home inspector) in desperation. The conversation went something like this:

"Hi, Aaron. I have a question for you."

"Shoot."

"I think I ran our well dry watering our lawn."

Confidently, Aaron answered, "No, you wouldn't have done that. It can handle it. How many hoses are you running?"

I gulped out, "Three. And I can't get any more water to come out."

Silence.

"Three? At the same time? . . . Yep, you ran it dry."

"Oh dear!" Now totally sick to my stomach, I quickly asked, "Will it be okay? What should I do now?"

"Just give it some time to refill and you'll be okay."

I turned everything off, prayed the water tables would refill, and waited. Thankfully, I did have water at the house again, but out of extra precaution, we didn't flush toilets or run any water for the rest of the evening.

I couldn't believe that my well ran dry. My resources had been depleted. The water was gone. But let me say this: you may be able to run a well dry, but God's resources will never run out. "Empty" is never a sticker to be slapped on His well of power and strength. His reserves will not run dry. When you feel like you are at the end of your rope, like you can climb no more hills, like you can weather no more valleys, His strength has no limits. Blessed are those whose strength is in Him! He will not fail you. He is all-sufficient. You can trust Him, rely on Him, and find your strength in Him.

> ✢**How does this bring you comfort and relief? Do you need this reminder today?**

In Psalm 84:5, finding our strength in Him is the first thing that brings blessing. What else brings the blessing of God according to this verse? The second thing we see is having a heart set on journey. As I mentioned in the introduction video, the Hebrew word for pilgrimage literally means "highway."[8] It is like the psalmist is saying the "highways are in their hearts."[9] Something common we see in the nature of the Hebrew language is to mix the actual and the figurative, "to present the spiritual side by side with the literal."[10]

The psalmist was physically on the road to Jerusalem heading to the courts of God, the dwelling place of the Lord Almighty. But even more amazing is that his heart was ready for the spiritual journey as well. He had it in his heart to seek God, to follow His ways, to go on an adventure, and trust that God would lead and direct.

This is the pilgrimage of life. Yes, there will be ups and downs. There will be high joys and deep lows. But this pilgrim saw the big picture and delighted in the highway—the path that God would take him on. A heart for journey truly is a perspective shift. It is seeing the journey as a whole, both in a reality as we know we are making our journey to Zion and one day, we will stand before Him literally, but also in how He will use this life now—our earthly journeys—to draw us closer to Him, to change us to look more like His Son, and to make a difference on this earth.

This perspective keeps an open heart to what God is doing—what He wants to do in you and through you, both today *and* tomorrow. A pilgrim perspective can put the events of the day in light of eternity and eternal significance. This kind of perspective sees a big, powerful, and living God who can be trusted—not only with life after death, but also with the life we live here until we arrive at our final destination.

The pilgrim's heart is set on a path where God leads and directs, where His voice is the loudest in the room, and in His presence, we find the greatest delight and the fullest of joys.

> A heart for journey is marked by a perspective that sees the big picture and a big God.

In what ways does the believer's perspective on journey differ from the world's perspective?

It is easy to get stuck along the side of the road and feel pressure from our culture. How are you doing with a heart for journey? What is your perspective?

Week One

Let's tackle two more verses in this Psalm today. Read Psalm 84:6–7. What was the pilgrim passing through and what did it become?

This Valley of Baka is an unknown place. The Bible makes no other reference to it. Some believe it was only a figurative place, but I don't see why it couldn't be real. The word baka (sometimes spelled baca) is associated with weeping.[11] It lends reference to the balsam tree, which had a sap that oozed like tears.[12]

Balsam trees favored dry and arid places. However, as the pilgrim passed through this parched valley, the landscape changed. The dusty valley became a place of springs, covered with pools from the autumn rains. It changed from terribly dry to marvelously hydrated. From lamentation and weeping to refreshment. From adversity to blessing.

One commentator noted that "faith turns it [the dehydrated valley] into a place of springs, finding refreshment under the most untoward circumstances . . . God refreshes them with showers of blessing from above."[13]

Isn't that like our God? He transforms the dry places of our lives into fountains, wells, and springs. He sends the autumn rains. The psalmist deliberately contrasted the dry valley and the transformation that brings relief and hope. One commentary even noted that the dry land became a land of springs "because of the faithful pilgrims' presence."[14] What a legacy that would be! The pilgrim didn't stay in the valley, but rather passed through it, receiving blessing and yet leaving a blessing behind as well.[15]

✢Have you ever known someone who could transform a desert into a garden? Jot down a few notes about him or her.

> "The desert and the parched land will be glad; the wilderness will rejoice and blossom. Like the crocus, it will burst into bloom; it will rejoice greatly and shout for joy . . . they will see the glory of the LORD, the splendor of our God. . . . Water will gush forth in the wilderness and streams in the desert. The burning sand will become a pool, the thirsty ground bubbling springs. In the haunts where the jackals once lay, grass and reeds and papyrus will grow."
>
> —ISAIAH 35:1–2, 6B-7

In verse 7, the psalmist mentioned that the traveler goes from strength to strength until ultimately appearing before God in Zion. As we journey, know that God gives strength for each task. And this strength builds because we are relying on Him.

Read Isaiah 40:28–31 below. Underline any key words and phrases that stand out to you.

Do you not know? Have you not heard? The LORD is the everlasting God, the Creator of the ends of the earth. He will not grow tired or weary, and his understanding no one can fathom. He gives strength to the weary and increases the power of the weak. Even youths grow tired and weary, and young men stumble and fall; but those who hope in the LORD will renew their strength. They will soar on wings like eagles; they will run and not grow weary, they will walk and not be faint.

How do you feel about journey now? We know the One who is with us. His promises are great, and they are true!

Ready to travel?

Day Five

In the corner of our basement, sits a little booth area with an "L" shaped bench, a round table for games, and several stools. The table is not a fancy table but rather an old, giant spool used for commercial electric wire—and I love it. It is rustic and rough-looking, and the best part is that it was free.

When we first brought it home, the wood was very coarse and splintery. But I sanded and sanded until the finish was smooth to the touch. After all, who wants a splinter while playing rummy or Apples to Apples? After the sanding, came the staining, but before applying a sealant, I added a little text to the top. I stenciled a boxy set of numbers for that industrial, shipping-like feel, including the date on which we moved into the house. I also painted the phrase "bendito viaje" which means "blessed journey" in Spanish. This is what I wanted our family perspective to be. I wanted to remember the building of our house, the finishing of the basement, our family life, and all the blessings God has given us. I wanted our lives in general to be marked with the phrase, "blessed journey." Despite the hard times, the rough seasons, the trials and tribulations (because we all know they happen!), I want my perspective and my heart to be set on the journey; a journey with the Lord that will be defined by Him, His great power, and what He wants to do in the lives of our family.

Our perspective strongly characterizes so much of our journey through this life, and yesterday, we talked about perspective being at the heart of journey. Right on the heels of perspective, however, are things like purpose and priorities. We'll talk about purpose next week, but for today, let's spend some time thinking about priorities.

What are your current priorities?

I like to think my priorities are good and well established, but sometimes I feel as if I have spread myself too thin, and that requires re-evaluating my priorities. The things that carry the most importance in our hearts should be reflected in what and where we spend our time. A look at our schedule reveals whether or not that actually holds true.

Does the way you spend your time reflect your most important priorities?

> ✣**Let's look at what the sons of Korah prioritized and how they concluded Psalm 84. Please read verses 8–12. What comparisons were made in verse 10, and what was prioritized?**

Now in verses 8 and 9, the psalmist asked God to hear his prayer and look with favor on His anointed one. Who is the shield and anointed one? After digging through different translations and commentaries, and sifting through whether the writer is referring to God as Israel's shield or the king God had placed over them, I do think this is a simple request for favor on their king.[16]

But then the writer transitioned to a statement of what he valued. The psalmist said that he would rather spend one day in the courts of the Lord than a thousand elsewhere. Imagine that! This is how he felt about being in God's dwelling place. It was that precious to him. It was that much of a privilege to be near to his God. Does that resound in your heart as well?

When I pause to think about the privileges we have as believers, I am in awe. Hebrews 4:16 tells us that we can come boldly before the throne and make our requests known to God. Because of what Jesus did for us on the cross, we have been given constant and consistent access to the living God. No other religious system offers this access, not to mention the ability to have a relationship with the one true Creator and Savior.

The psalmist longed to be near God. He would rather spend one day in His presence than a thousand elsewhere. He treasured God's presence. In fact, he even said he would rather be a doorkeeper in the house of his God than dwell in the tents of the wicked. A doorkeeper. Even being at the threshold of God's dwelling place was prized by this writer. Incidentally, does that phrase "dwell in the tents of the wicked" sound familiar?

> **If not, take a look back at Numbers 16:26–27. Who was this in reference to?**

Allow me to ask you a few questions:

Do you treasure your devotional time with the Lord and in His Word?

Do you see prayer as a blessing and a joy?

Do you consider being able to worship with a community of faith a privilege?

The value you place on these things will define how much you prioritize them in your life. Your view of God's Word, of prayer, and of church life affects the energy you put into them. If you think highly of prayer, if you believe it works, and that it helps you grow closer to God, you will make time for it in your life (and likewise with studying God's Word).

When I hear the stories of Christians around the world being persecuted for their faith, I am reminded of how incredibly blessed we are to be able to freely worship our God in the U.S.A. But do I treat it like the blessing it is? How easy it can be to take for granted the ability to worship without fear while others around the world are forced to meet in secret.

List a few things that we tend to take advantage of as believers in this part of the world.

Glance back to Psalm 84:3. Who made a home at the tabernacle?

The psalmist envied these sweet little birds and those who were able to dwell in God's house, those who made the tabernacle their home. There is great importance in becoming deeply involved in a Bible-teaching community of faith. I am so grateful for my church and the fact that my children feel at home there.

> **Like the sparrow of Psalm 84, have you nested at church? Have you become involved and tied to a local congregation of believers?**

I can't tell you how important it is to find a church and connect with other believers there. I know God is everywhere (including your living room), but He instructs us to not forsake gathering together (Heb. 10:25). Over the last few years, so many have gone without church. Online church is no replacement for actually worshipping together, sharing needs, supporting each other, and fellowshipping together. You need the church and the church needs you.

Incidentally, I am not so naïve as to think that some of us haven't experienced deep heartache within church walls. But please don't give up on it! God's design is for us to be in communities of faith.

> **Do you make church a priority? _____**

> **If you have children, do your children know that church is a priority over worldly activities? Is your church a home to them? If not, what will you do about it?**

Did you happen to notice that Psalm 84 contains three statements of blessing? In fact, dwelling in God's house is what prompts the first of the three "blessed are" statements found in this psalm.

> **Can you find the others? Blessed are . . .**
>
> **Verse 4: those who dwell in Your house**
>
> **Verse 5:**
>
> **Verse 12:**

✣ Is there one that needs to be better developed in your life?

The psalmist went on to share in verse 11 that the Lord is a sun and shield. The Lord is a sun in the sense that He is a light and direction to those who look to Him. When we are in the dark, He is the light. He illuminates, enlightens, leads, and guides.

The Lord is also a shield, protecting us along the way. We are safe in Him. Nothing will happen to us that He hasn't allowed. Please note that the psalmist didn't say that He is *sometimes* a sun and shield. Rather, he said the Lord *is* a sun and shield. God is intentional with the traveler and the psalmist knew it. He directs and protects. He did this for the Israelite traveling to Jerusalem, and He will do this for you. You aren't alone. God is with you the whole way. He gives grace and glory, favor and honor. No good thing is withheld from those who are blameless. Now this doesn't mean we get everything we want. But it does mean God does not withhold what is for our good. And we need not worry about this but can rest in the faithfulness and character of our loving God. Once again, He is trustworthy. And the final verse reminds us of this—the third statement of blessing—"Blessed is the one who trusts in you" Psalm 84:12.

As we finish our first week together, take some time to draw near to God. Go with the sons of Korah to Jerusalem. Make the journey—remembering that your path is not defined by anyone or anything other than your God. Remember the importance in seeking after God and developing a passion for His presence. Find comfort in the fact that His strength does not run dry. And know that our perspective and priorities will impact the path we take and the joy we experience along the way. As we are faithful to develop our heart for journey, we will see God stretch us, bless us, and open our eyes to the possibilities of a life lived with Him. To Him be all glory!

Next week, we'll discover more of what it means to have a heart for journey as we study the book of Ezra. While Amos looked toward the imminent exile of the northern and southern kingdoms, Ezra will take us journeying back home to Jerusalem.

> *"It was the LORD our God himself who brought us and our parents up out of Egypt, from that land of slavery, and performed those great signs before our eyes. He protected us on our entire journey and among all the nations through which we traveled."*
>
> —JOSHUA 24:17

WATCH THE WEEK 1 VIDEO

Line of Sight

Scriptures in this Session: Matthew 14:22–33, John 6:14–15

Also mentioned: Job 9:8, Exodus 3:14, Hebrews 11:6, 2 Timothy 1:7

Whether it is a moment of chaos or concern, we need to _____ _____ with the Father who loves us.

It is much better to be in _____ _____ when rough waters come, than in the land of our own ideas, aspirations, and goals.

The reason we can have courage and be of good cheer has nothing to do with _____ and everything to do with _____.

Don't be afraid to ask for the audacious when it is asked in sincere and genuine _____.

For the Christian, line of sight is not only an unobstructed view, but also an _____ view.

Video lessons are available at KristenTiber.com/AHeartForJourneyVideos.

Week Two

A Return Trip

*"For it is God who works in you
to will and to act in order to
fulfill his good purpose."*

PHILIPPIANS 2:13

Day One

Welcome back for week 2! This week, we will be studying another traveler of the Old Testament—a man who devoted himself to the Lord, His Word, and His people. This man led a large contingency of Israelites on a journey back to the city of God's dwelling place following the exile. His name? Ezra.

Oh, how I love the books of Ezra and Nehemiah, and the accounts within: stirring stories of God moving the hearts of kings, people deeply convicted to rebuilding Jerusalem, and individuals who desired to lift up the name of Yahweh once again in the land. Ah, the heart for restoration! Don't get me wrong—there's bad stuff too. People sin and opposition arises. But God remains faithful through it all, and we see some amazing things happen.

Let's set the stage. The northern kingdom had been taken into exile while Jeroboam II was in charge. In 605 BC, Nebuchadnezzar, ruler of Babylon, deported Judah's royal family from the southern kingdom and took vessels from the temple in Jerusalem. In 597 BC, he began to exile the fighting men and craftsmen.[17] In 586 BC, Nebuchadnezzar all out attacked and destroyed Jerusalem, including the temple the Israelites loved so very much. Most of the Jews were then taken off to Babylon, a city of great sin and idolatry. During their exile however, we read the heroic and faith-building accounts of people like Daniel in the lion's den, Shadrach, Meshach, and Abednego in the fiery furnace, and Esther and Mordecai. Yes, even in Babylon, God was moving. The chosen people were not alone, and a faithful remnant could still be found.

> *"[The Lord] who says of Cyrus, 'He is my shepherd and will accomplish all that I please; he will say of Jerusalem, "Let it be rebuilt," and of the temple, "Let its foundations be laid."'"*
>
> —ISAIAH 44:28

Isaiah had prophesied about the exile (Isa. 6:11–12, 39:5–7), but he also prophesied about their return to Jerusalem. Read Isaiah 44:28 in the margin. In the year 538 BC, Cyrus the Great (the King of Persia who had conquered Babylon) issued a decree that allowed the Israelites to return to their homeland. And so fifty thousand Jews made the four-month journey home with Zerubbabel, head of the tribe of Judah, to reestablish Jerusalem and rebuild the temple.[18]

Where we will pick up in our story today is the year 458 BC when Ezra was about to return to Jerusalem with a second round of exiles heading home. The temple had been rebuilt (516 BC), but there was still much work remaining in the restoration of Israel, both physically and spiritually.

Read Ezra 7:1–11. Who was the King of Persia at this time?

⁜Write down everything you can about the man Ezra. (While you don't need to list all of his ancestors, please note to whom Ezra is able to trace his lineage.)

What did the king grant Ezra (verse 6)?

Twice in this passage, it is noted that something was upon Ezra. What was it?

King Artaxerxes I was ruler of Persia when Ezra returned to Jerusalem. What did you write down about Ezra? Did you note that he was a descendant of Aaron, the chief priest and brother of Moses? One thing I love is that even while exiled in Babylon, there were still people studying God's Word. There was a faithful remnant and Ezra was among them. In fact, I would venture to say that based on his standing with the king, Ezra stood out among the others. He was a priest, well versed in the Law of Moses, and devoted to the study, teaching, and observance of the law.

As we will see this week, Ezra loved the Lord and desired to see Him exalted. I imagine his heart ached for the restoration of the Holy City and the chosen people of his God. Ezra was called by the Lord to a great journey—although not an easy journey. Many Jews had chosen to remain in Babylon. I wonder if life was too comfortable for them. But Ezra—full of passion and purpose, and experiencing the hand of God—knew it was time to go home.

We see several times that the Scriptures tell us that God's hand was upon Ezra. We read it and Ezra acknowledges it. The phrase appears six times in Ezra 7 and 8. What do you think it means that God's hand was upon Ezra? In various places in the Scriptures, we read about God's hand being upon a particular individual or group of people. Sometimes it was a good thing as in the case for Nehemiah, Elisha, and Ezekiel. However at other times, it was a bad thing when God's hand was against the Egyptians, Bar-Jesus, and even the Israelites at times. Either way, this phrase always demonstrated the power and intention of the Almighty. In Ezra's case, it was the favor of God backed by His mighty power.

If Ezra remained faithful to the Lord, God would carry him through every hilltop, every valley, and every challenge. Ezra would know God's favor and power in whatever he was doing. And how important this was! The 900-mile journey[19] wouldn't be easy, and neither would the task of restoring Israel.

The "destination" or measure of success of Ezra's journey wouldn't simply be planting his feet on the dirt of Jerusalem. No, the real work would begin for Ezra when he arrived. But God's hand would be upon this priest, giving favor and direction all along the way. And that would also be the case once again with Nehemiah as we will see later when he asks the Persian king to allow him to go and rebuild the walls around the Holy City. Have you experienced the gracious hand of God upon you? It is a beautiful and powerful thing.

✢Recall a time when you experienced His favor.

Take a moment now and read the sending letter that King Artaxerxes prepared for Ezra in verses 12–26. Write down anything that stands out to you.

Wow! Do you think God's hand was upon Ezra with such a letter? I'm pretty impressed with this king and his generous inclination to help Ezra in such a way. How gracious was the hand of God!

In verse 14, who was identified as sending Ezra?

According to the letter, Ezra was being sent by King Artaxerxes and his seven advisers. These men made great strides at providing the Israelites with an abundance of supplies and gifts, even to the point of mandating others in the Trans-Euphrates to help as well. Although in God's sovereignty, we know the Lord was the ultimate sender and the One bringing His people home with such bounty. Let's take a look at other examples in the Bible of people being sent out for a purpose. The examples are numerous, but we will just look at two.

Read Luke 9:1–6 and Luke 22:7–13. In both cases, answer these three questions: Who was the sender? Who was sent? Why were they sent?

When I tell my kids to go outside and play, it is never without reason. I have most likely sent them out to get some fresh air in their bodies, some sun on their faces, or even a refreshed mindset. When they were younger, it may have also been so I could get something done.

> Whenever there is a sender, there is a purpose.

Whenever there is a sender, there is a purpose. Every time we read of a journey in the Bible—whether a grand trip or less significant task—there is a purpose. For Ezra, it was the restoration of Jerusalem and her people. For the twelve disciples, it was evangelism and ministry work. For Peter and John, it was to prepare the Passover. Whenever someone is sent, there is always a reason.

Like Ezra and the disciples, you too have a sender on your journey in this life. But He is much more than the king of an earthly empire or its human advisors. Your sender is the Creator of the Universe, the living God, and the Lord Almighty. You are His chosen daughter. He has adopted you into His family. He sees you, knows you, and values you. His blessing accompanies you, and in Him, you are more than a conqueror.* His sending letter is His Word and you are not without purpose. In fact, the Father in His wisdom, weaves purpose through every season you face. Every season!

> *See Ephesians 1:4–5, 11, Genesis 16:13, Jeremiah 1:5, Romans 8:37

Recently, I was facing something challenging and well, lengthy. The situation was weighing so heavily on my mind, it became a rather large focus of my time and energy. But I had to force myself to try to put it into perspective. How did God want me to handle this? What purpose did this challenge serve in my life? Truthfully, I wanted to say, "None!" It was just a lousy situation, and I couldn't wait to be past it. But I had to ask—would God be faithful to make use of even this? Oh yes. Yes, He would. And He will for whatever you're facing too.

When you are tempted to want to wash away the season you are in, remember that God will bring purpose into it. Whether He is drawing you closer to Him, helping you grow, or imparting strength and faith, there will always be a purpose. What might you learn? How will He show Himself faithful?

Are you currently dealing with something difficult? Have you stopped to think of how God will use it—how He will weave purpose into the season? How might this draw you closer to Him or grow you in your faith?

I know in the toughest of situations, it can be hard to see that God could bring any purpose into the circumstance. But trust Him to be with you and to be at work. If you are sad, let Him minister to your heart as you run to the shadow of His wings. If you are discouraged, lift up your head and see how big your God is. Open your eyes and watch for His work. My dear sister, know that there is purpose in every season. It may be hard to see, but it is there. You might not see it right away, but God is at work in you. You are His beloved child.

> A heart for journey believes there is purpose in every season.

As we wrap up today's lesson, read Ezra 7:27–28. What was Ezra's response to the king's letter?

Ah, I love this. It is so beautiful. Ezra first praised God. He recognized the Lord's hand upon them. And then what was the result? Courage. Ezra "took courage and gathered leaders from Israel to go up with [him]" (Ezra 7:28).

Take courage, my friend. When you are seeking God and following His ways, His hand will be upon you. You will be able to take the next step—whether it is a step towards Jerusalem or into the unknown of what lies ahead for you. God's purpose will always prevail (Prov. 19:21).

Day Two

Let's jump right back in and look again at the King of Persia's letter in Ezra 7:12–26. What was given to the group of exiles returning to Jerusalem?

Fifteen hundred men (plus women and children) accompanied Ezra to the city of David.[20] The path they travelled was about 900 miles and took four months.[21] And after everything the king sent, they certainly carried more than just their own belongings. King Artaxerxes offered gold and silver from the royal treasury and from the province of Babylon. He asked the people to give free will offerings. The exiles also took with them the remaining articles of the temple that hadn't already been sent back with Zerubbabel in chapter one of the book of Ezra.

And as if that wasn't enough, the king decreed that the treasurers of the Trans-Euphrates were to give Ezra whatever he asked of them up to a set amount. In our own measurements, this means they could have been carrying nearly four tons of silver,[22] eighteen tons of wheat, and about six hundred gallons of wine and olive oil each![23] Do you think they had a good amount of provisions given to them?

> "Where God's agenda is championed, God's resources flow."
>
> —CHIP INGRAM[24]

I remember when Dan and I took the kids on a mid-week getaway to a friend's house in Lake Chautauqua, New York. It was when they were small and still in diapers. The amount of stuff we packed was ridiculous. Granted we had to take food, towels, and other supplies, but the baby and toddler items—yikes! Our car was full, and we were only gone for a few days.

Artaxerxes was exceedingly generous, especially given the fact that he had nothing in particular to gain from the Israelites' departure. Yet, incredible provisions were made. And while Artaxerxes sent the people to Jerusalem, ultimately we know he was being used by God as the instrument by which the Lord would bring His people out of exile as promised. Oh yes, God provided what was needed to fulfill what He promised. And He still does that today.

> "Which of you, if your son asks for bread, will give him a stone? Or if he asks for a fish, will give him a snake? If you, then, though you are evil, know how to give good gifts to your children, how much more will your Father in heaven give good gifts to those who ask him!"
>
> —MATTHEW 7:9–11

Let's hop back to Genesis 22 and read another story about God's provision. This time it wasn't a massive number of people taking a long trip, but rather a simple father and his precious son on a three-day journey.[25]

Turn to Genesis 22 and read verses 1–14. How did God test Abraham?

What was provided in Isaac's place?

✤**What did Abraham call that place (verse 14)?**

From this account is where we get the name for God, *Jehovah Jireh* or in Hebrew, *Yahweh Yireh*. This is the only place in Scripture that the name appears yet consider how well-known and important this title is. It has brought comfort and peace to countless believers.

✤**Think of a time when God has provided for you and record it below.**

Let's look at a couple of things about Yahweh Yireh. First, I would like us to notice the tense of this name. It isn't in the past tense where God provid*ed*. It isn't even in the present tense with God provid*ing*. Yahweh Yireh is in the future tense—God *will* provide.[26] Abraham has made this statement *after* God provided the ram, and so this declaration is bursting with realized confidence and faith in the fact that not only does God provide, but also that He will always provide! Oh, how I wonder how the name of this site encouraged other travelers in their own situations!

✤**How does knowing that God *will* provide bring you comfort?**

Second, let's look more closely at what Yahweh Yireh means. The name is given by Abraham to the place where God provided a ram as a substitutional sacrifice for his son, Isaac. But the meaning is a little more complicated than it appears in the English as "[t]he LORD will provide." With a little digging, we will discover that the name reveals something so very beautiful about the character and nature of God.

Have you ever looked up a word from the Bible in the original Greek or Hebrew? It is actually a very easy process online. With just a couple of clicks, such depth can be added to whatever you are reading.

One day after hearing a message on Genesis 22, I was curious to see verse 14 in the Hebrew. I keep an app called BibleHub on my phone for cases like this. With a few clicks, I was looking at the Hebrew word translated for us as "provide" and saw that it was *yireh*. (The letter J doesn't exist in the Hebrew language, so when you hear a J sound in English, it is usually the Y sound in Hebrew. Jehovah Jireh . . . Yahweh Yireh.)

As I looked further, much to my dismay, I found that the initial, short definition of yireh said nothing about providing. Instead, what I discovered is that the word yireh is primarily defined as "to see." This was completely confusing! Pastors and Bible teachers couldn't have been getting it wrong all these years. There had to be more to it so I continued to research.

Here is what I learned: A fuller definition of the word denotes, "to see, look, view, to realize, know, consider . . . to become visible, appear, show oneself."[27] Lexical aids add, "to understand intellectually, perceive . . . to attend to."[28] So while the word means "to see," it is more than just visual sight. And some of the sources did include "provide" lower in the definition listing.

So how do we reconcile Yahweh Yireh as the Lord who will *provide*? Here is what we have to remember: the names and titles that God shared and that people used often rose out of the particular situation. We cannot separate the revealed name from the event at hand. The account in Genesis hinges on the fact that God provided a ram in Isaac's place.

We also must remember the nature of our God. He is God Almighty—omnipotent, omniscient, and omnipresent. He is the God who sees and perceives. And the beauty of this word, yireh, is that you can't separate His seeing from His providing. The Lord sees, knows, and attends to our situation as we saw in the definition above. He foresees the need and in advance, He makes provisions. And He does this before we are even aware of our need.[29]

Check out what Nathan Stone says in his book, *Names of God*:

> . . . with God, **to see is also to foresee**. As the One who possesses eternal wisdom and knowledge, He knows the end from the beginning. As Elohim He is all-knowing, all-wise, and all-powerful. From eternity to eternity He foresees everything. . . . **Thus with God foreseeing is prevision**. As the Jehovah of righteousness and holiness, and of love and redemption, having prevision of man's sin, and fall, and need, **He makes provision for that need**. For provision, after all, is merely a compound of two Latin words meaning "to see beforehand." And we may learn from a dictionary that *provide* is simply the verb and *prevision* the noun of seeing beforehand. **Thus to God prevision is necessarily followed by provision**, for He certainly will provide for that need that His foreseeing shows Him to exist. **With Him prevision and provision is one and the same thing.**[30] [emphasis added]

Whoosh! Is your head spinning? What is your take on this?

If I know my child is going to be hungry when he gets home from basketball, and I have a snack ready for him, I have provided for him based on what I foresaw would happen. God provided what He foresaw was needed for Abraham. Human sacrifice was a pagan practice and its forbiddance later became part of the Hebrew laws. Although, don't you wonder what was going through Abraham's head? I do think he was either trusting the character of God to stop the sacrifice or the power of God to resurrect a sacrificed son. Whichever, I think he still believed Isaac was the child of the promise. What makes me think this? Did you catch that he told his servants, "We will worship and then **we** will come back to you" (Gen. 22:5)? [emphasis added]

In the provision of the ram, God foreshadowed the model of animal substitution that would come with Moses and the sacrificial system. But we would be remiss not to also see the bigger picture here. This entire scene was a foreshadowing of the greater substitution that God would provide for us in His Son Jesus. Romans 8:32 says, "He who did not spare his own Son, but gave him up for us all—how will he not also, along with him, graciously give us all things?"

Oh yes, our God is the great provider. Whether we're talking about goods for the journey, a ram for Abraham and Isaac, or the very Son of God for a beloved people precious to the Creator, Yahweh Yireh is the provider. He sees, and He provides. Not just anything we want, but what He determines we need. When you have a need, God sees the need and He will provide from whatever source pleases Him—whether the king of a large empire or a ram in the thicket—even to the point of His own Son. Jesus is the greatest provision ever made and it was made for you and for me! To the praise of His glory!

What is your current need? The Lord sees your situation and has already put the plans in place to provide. Prevision and provision. Feels like a pretty safe place to be on the journey. Thank you, Lord!

> A heart for journey has confidence that the Lord sees and will provide for any needs along the way.

What is your need right now?

Thank Him for being your provider in the space below.

Day Three

In 1969, Buzz Aldrin and Neil Armstrong were the first men to set foot on the moon. As millions around the globe tuned in, and Neil Armstrong stepped off the ladder of the Eagle onto the surface of the moon, he spoke the words that have since been revered for such a momentous occasion, "One small step for man; one giant leap for mankind."

Today, we are going to talk about the topic of faith. Because any journey—whether a monumental life change or just an ordinary day around the sun—requires faith. And sometimes that faith is just a small step. But at other times, it's a giant leap. Let's see what Ezra faced as we explore chapter eight.

Read Ezra 8:15–21. What did Ezra do before leaving Babylon?

This chapter starts with a list of family heads that went with Ezra back to Jerusalem. Then as Ezra was assembling the people, he discovered that there weren't any Levites among them. Levites would be needed to serve in the temple, so Ezra sent out a team of men to recruit the priestly tribe. And because the gracious hand of God was upon them, the group brought back thirty-eight Levites and 220 temple servants (those who assisted Levites).

Once the Levites joined them, however, Ezra didn't rush to get on the road like I would have wanted to do. No, he did something else first. He proclaimed a fast. But this fast was not just for himself; he called on the entire company of Israelites to humble themselves before the Lord. They prayed and asked the Lord for a safe journey before leaving.

Ezra knew the people were supposed to go back to the Holy Land, the land promised to the Hebrews. He knew they were in the will of God, yet they still fasted and prayed. Why? Because there is something so important about humility before God, and this can be one of the hardest spiritual characteristics to possess and maintain.

You might wonder if humility is so important, how can we go boldly before the throne (as we talked about in the first week)? The answer is that we can go boldly before the throne not because of who we are or what we have done, but rather because Jesus has paid the way for our access to the Father. When we go boldly, we still kneel. We still humble ourselves. We would be wise to humble ourselves not just before we take a big step or new direction in life, but also daily before our God.

> ✣ **Think of someone you know who is humble. What do you notice about his or her heart?**

> **Read Ezra 8:22–23. Why didn't Ezra ask the king for armed guards for their long trip?**

The road from Mesopotamia to Jerusalem was a dangerous road, filled with bandits and thieves. The journey was not an easy one. It was risky. It was unsafe. In a later journey from Babylon, Nehemiah accepted the armed escort sent by the king (Neh. 2:9). Here though, Ezra debated on asking King Artaxerxes for a security detail. But he decided not to. Scripture tells us that Ezra felt ashamed to ask the king. Why? Ezra had been telling the king already that God's gracious hand was upon him. To ask the king to provide security, would be to tell the king that he didn't trust God to carry out the task and to protect them on their journey.

Have you ever felt like that before? Wanting to trust that God is who He says He is and able to do anything? Wanting to have a big faith, but still desiring to implement safeguards around you?

Have you ever wanted to provide your own safeguards instead of relying on God? Share an example below.

Ezra decided to walk in faith. And when he took the first step (or even that giant leap) away from the Ahava Canal, after having fasted and prayed, Ezra and the 1,500+ Hebrews with him took the journey in faith. They believed that the gracious hand of God would continue to be upon them as long as they didn't forsake Him. They put their faith in a God whom millions had before and were not disappointed. God was enough.

Reread verse 23. What did God do?

✣**Do you need to take a step of faith, or maybe even a leap? What are the circumstances?**

Will you trust God and believe that He is faithful? Have you brought your need before Him? Journal your thoughts here.

Recently, I ran into a woman I used to know from my previous church. We had been in a prayer ministry together—one with the specific mission of praying for and reaching out to the unsaved in our own personal circles of influence. She shared with me that a co-worker was going through a difficult time so she sent a card with a Bible verse and a note that she was praying for her. It was a simple step of faith and seemed well enough received. Not too long after though, this same co-worker told another co-worker about my friend's faith and prayers, and encouraged her to talk to my friend. The woman came and asked my friend for prayer as well! Look at what came from a simple step of faith.

Curious what happens next in the account of Ezra and the Israelites? Read Ezra 8:24–36 to finish the chapter. What was the outcome of the trip?

There will be many things that people put their trust in: money, material goods, power, influence, good health, even follower counts on social media. . . . What do you put your trust in? What or who will carry you safely through this journey? I hope it is Ezra's faithful God. What's pretty amazing is that the God who parts the rivers and seas, who thwarts the attack of enemies, and answers the prayers of simple men, He is your God too. He has an incredible past, and always remember that He holds *your* future.

> *"Some trust in chariots and some in horses, but we trust in the name of the LORD our God."*
>
> —PSALM 20:7

Day Four

Oh boy! Things were looking so promising, were they not as we closed out chapter eight? The Israelites had arrived in Jerusalem. God had kept them safe. The people offered sacrifices at the temple rebuilt by Zerubbabel, and they were even receiving assistance from local governors and leaders (thanks to the letter sent by King Artaxerxes). For the Israelites, the excitement must have been thrilling—they were home! They were back. They had a temple, and God was moving. But unfortunately, so were the disobedient hearts of men.

Read Ezra 9:1–2. What had some of the Israelites done? And which leaders were included in this group?

Time had passed (another four months)[31] and some of the Israelites mixed with other cultures and took foreign wives. Why was this a problem?

Read Exodus 34:15–16 and Deuteronomy 7:1–6. Why weren't the Israelites supposed to intermarry?

Israel was God's chosen nation. They hadn't done anything to earn this choosing. According to Deuteronomy 7:7–9, the Lord chose them and set His affection on them not because they were more numerous than other nations, but because the Lord loved them and kept His covenant of love and oath to their ancestors. The people of Israel were to remain a pure nation, a holy people—set apart because their God was holy. Marriage to foreigners who worshipped other gods over and over again led Israel into idolatry.

This was no small matter. What the people did here was grievous to the Lord! Some Israelites even divorced their Jewish wives in order to marry foreign women (Mal. 2:10–16).[32] And after Ezra learned of what they had done, he was appalled.

Read Ezra's response in Ezra 9:3–6a. What did Ezra do?

"Be holy because I am holy."

—LEVITICUS 11:44

Ezra's response is a lesson for us all. We have forgotten how to blush in the world today. Sin and evil used to be an embarrassment. One week, my pastor shared this quote from an unknown author, "First, we overlook evil. Then, we permit evil. Then, we legalize evil. Then, we promote evil. Then, we celebrate evil. Then, we persecute those who still call it evil." Or check out what Mark Dever said, "Sin once tolerated, seeks to be accepted, and sin once accepted, seeks to be celebrated."[33] Throughout history, this has been the case. But if you're like me, something today seems more backwards than ever before in our lifetime. God has standards and whether they are the big things or even the small things (as if there were a difference—it is all sin), we have forgotten He is holy and asks us to be holy as well.

⁜What is our culture's response to sin?

What is your response to your own sin?

As a follower of Christ, you are called to obedience and a holy life. Do you live like someone set apart or do you live like the rest of the world? Do your co-workers recognize something different about you because of your language and the choices you make? Do your friends and neighbors see a set of priorities and actions founded on something other than self or worldly gain? We live in a very anti-God climate. A believer who loves the Lord and tries to live a holy life stands out! How could she not? But be sure that when you stand out, you do so with grace and truth (John 1:14). Both are required to reflect Christ in what we say and do.

I often wonder if one of the reasons people don't want to admit or consider the existence of God is because we have always desired to be in charge of our own lives. To believe in God, One who created everything we see in nature, means there is someone to whom we answer. There is someone greater than us. And if this is the case, we will have to follow what He says. Our autonomous society doesn't like that idea.

Even though we as Christians are called to obedience, let's remember that it isn't to an unjust dictator. Neither is this a robotic act of submission. No, it is something much different. It is something that starts in our heart.

Turn to John 14:15. What does Jesus say we will do if we love Him?

The God we obey is a just and loving God. And the kind of love He has for us is this, "For God so loved the world that He gave His one and only Son, that whoever believes in Him shall not perish but have eternal life" (John 3:16). He loves us sacrificially and with our best always in mind. His laws, statutes, and yes, rules are always for our good. They are protections set up for our whole-person health—physically, spiritually, mentally, and emotionally. They are for our welfare. And when we consider who He is and what He has done, my hope is that our hearts overflow with love and appreciation—and because we love Him, then we obey Him.

Read Ezra's prayer in Ezra 9:6–15. Make note of anything that stands out to you.

"Restore us to yourself, LORD, that we may return; renew our days as of old."

—LAMENTATIONS 5:21

Even though Ezra had nothing to do with the sin, he came before God to pray and confess corporately. Ezra recognized that sin is what sent Israel into captivity in the first place. They had not been an obedient people. They had not acted like God's treasured possession. And this led them into exile. Oh how Ezra must have been concerned they would head right back to Babylon. Blasted sin!

On our own journeys as followers of Christ, we need to strive to live according to biblical precepts. Sin hurts our walk with the Lord and pulls us away from fellowship with Him. On-going sin always leads to captivity. It starts small, but then as you give the enemy a foothold, it grows and grows, and eventually, it becomes a stronghold. Is there sin in your life that you need to confess and repent from? Can you take a cue from Ezra, humble yourself, and bring it before the Lord? No more avoiding. No more willful disobedience.

Is there sin you need to confess? Do you need to repent?

Now, what happened with Israel's sin? Did God send them right back to Babylon?

Read Ezra 10:1–6. What did the men, women, and children do who joined Ezra?

I love that the people told Ezra there was still hope for Israel, despite their unfaithfulness to the Lord. Do you need to hear that for yourself? You may have been visiting the foreign cities, making all kinds of bad choices, and moving away from God's will for your life, but there is still hope.

Tomorrow, we will look more at the exiles' return to Jerusalem with Nehemiah. But let's just take a sneak peek and see what Nehemiah prayed in chapter one.

Read Nehemiah 1:8–9 in the margin. What is the promise in this verse?

> "Remember the instruction you gave your servant Moses, saying, 'If you are unfaithful, I will scatter you among the nations, but if you return to me and obey my commands, then even if your exiled people are at the farthest horizon, I will gather them from there and bring them to the place I have chosen as a dwelling for my Name.'"
>
> —Nehemiah 1:8–9

Oh praise His name! Have you been in exile? Are you ready to return to Him? When your foot gets off the path, return. When your heart runs astray, return. When your mind is going to unhealthy places, return.

Return quickly. His promise is for you too. He will gather us back and bring us to the place of His dwelling. We can have restoration and renewed fellowship with the Lord. He has called you to walk set apart, to live well, and to flourish as His treasured possession. You are His chosen daughter, and His Name is upon you. On *His* path, you will grow in godliness, not the other way around. Reject sinful ways, and let Him mold you to look more like Jesus. That is the path. That is the way.

✣**How does the account and heart of Ezra instruct, encourage, or challenge you?**

Day 5

> A heart for journey knows the road that leads to captivity. Sin pulls us off the best path and hurts our walk with the Lord. A heart for journey, when getting off track, returns quickly.

Great job this week! As we wrap up week 2, we have talked about quite a bit as the exiles journeyed home to Jerusalem. We explored the fact that there is purpose in every season of our journey and that our God sees and provides for our needs. We saw that sometimes we need to take a step of faith, as well as how important obedience is in our walk. Today, we will look at what to do when opposition arises.

When we finished yesterday, Ezra and a team of Israelites were about to deal with the disobedience of the men who married foreign, pagan women. The guilty parties did admit their sin when confronted and the women were sent back home. Sin sure does have a way of affecting more than just the one who committed the offense, doesn't it?

Now, we are going to jump forward about fourteen years after Ezra's return. Nehemiah, an Israelite for whom I have so much respect and admiration, has come to Israel with the burden on his heart of rebuilding the wall that surrounded, fortified, and protected Jerusalem. It was quite an arduous task, and yet once again God had His hand upon our traveler. But even with the favor of God upon Nehemiah and the people, they still faced opposition.

Read Nehemiah 4:1–5. Who opposed the rebuilding of the wall? What was the first thing that Nehemiah did in response?

When faced with opposition, did Nehemiah retaliate? Did he hurl down insults against his opponents? Did he run to his fellow Israelites and conspire? No, he did not. Instead, he prayed. Throughout the whole book of Nehemiah, the importance of prayer is a prevalent theme. Now, was Nehemiah merciful in his prayer? No. He asked God for exactly what was on his mind. But let's save that for another study.

Read Nehemiah 4:6–12. Record Nehemiah's response in verse 9.

Again, we see Nehemiah praying. And this time, he also took action by posting a guard for protection. The Israelites were experiencing trouble. They had taken on an incredibly difficult task. The walls were in ruins. The city was broken down. The work was long and hard, and now enemies were rising up. In verse

10, we see that the Israelites were tired and discouraged, and in the following verse, we learn how fearful they were. And fear was multiplying as others talked about getting attacked. What a hard and challenging season in which to live!

When you are faced with opposition, how do you handle it?

Read Nehemiah 4:13–14. What did Nehemiah do to encourage the people?

Fill in the blank from verse 14:

"Remember the _____, who is _____ and _____."

Just as Nehemiah and the Israelites experienced difficulty, we too will face hard seasons and tough roads on our journey. No one gets through this life without them. Because of sin, the fact that we have an enemy, and that we live in a fallen world, without question, there will be rough spots. And sometimes, they will be excruciating.

Nevertheless, Nehemiah reminded the people to remember how great and awesome the Lord was. Nehemiah gave them perspective. Any problem shrinks in comparison to the One who set the stars in their place and tells the ocean when to move. When we can remember how powerful and mighty our God is, we are better able to put our situation into perspective. And perspective is so important, isn't it? It not only helps our problems to look smaller in light of the greatness of God, but it also helps us realize that more might be at play than what meets the eye.

Several years ago, I had a dream that I was standing in a grassy area, alongside a driveway. People kept coming up to me and harassing me. They were not physically bothering me, but they were verbally plaguing me. It was horrible. One after another, they came up to harass me. And one by one, I had to call on the name of Jesus, rebuke them, and tell them to go. And they did.

I shared that dream with a couple of people—with Dan, with my mom, and with a friend. But it wasn't until about six months later when I started having annoying health issues, my father-in-law became seriously sick, other family members were facing difficult challenges, one of my kids was struggling through something, there was a problem for my husband at work . . . it wasn't until I remembered that dream that I started *praying* like I was being harassed by the enemy. I had to change my perspective as to what I was facing. I had to see it for what it was. Satan, the roaring lion seeking to rob, kill, and destroy, had to be put in his place (1 Peter 5:8, John 10:10). I had to pray and stand my ground.

The God we serve is powerful. The name of Jesus is powerful! Know that you serve a mighty God who can do anything. God is bigger than whatever you are facing. He is more powerful than your situation and your opposition.

After the reminder of who God was, Nehemiah then encouraged the people to be strong and persevere. They needed to fight for their families. Do you need this reminder right now?

�֍How has remembering who God is in the midst of a trial or difficult situation bolstered your ability to handle the challenge?

✣**Let's read the rest of the chapter. Read Nehemiah 4:15–23. How did the men work according to verses 17–18?**

What an image to remember! Isn't this an allegory for so much of our lives? I have taught through Nehemiah a couple of times in moms' Bible studies and I love utilizing this image when it comes to how we raise our kids. We do the work of parenting with one hand while holding a weapon in the other—and that is because we are in a battle for our children's hearts and minds. During our study I even brought in a hammer and a sword so a mom could stand up and take the position. It made it so much easier to visualize and remember the lesson. But this doesn't just represent motherhood, it is a picture for our spiritual life.

When we are doing the work to which God has called us, when we are following, yielding, and passionate about Him, we will face opposition. There will be seasons when we hold our hammer and our sword, and are prepared to fight the enemy—whether it is the enemy of our own mind or the enemy of our souls—whether it is the world's anti-God direction where we strive to be salt and light or it is the battle for our own hearts and those of our children. Make no mistake, battles are fought on many fronts. But we have a God who equips us for battle.

Turn to Ephesians 6:10–18 to read about the armor of God. What is the one offensive weapon listed and what does Paul say it is (verse 17b)?

In Scripture, we are told that the weapons of our warfare are not carnal, but mighty in power to demolish strongholds (2 Cor. 10:4–5). According to what we just read, we battle not against flesh and blood, but against the rulers, authorities, dark powers, and spiritual forces of evil (Eph. 6:12). But we are equipped for battle with the full armor of God and with the sword of the Spirit, which is the Word of God, the Bible. How important it is then to know your Bible! This is our offensive weapon against the enemy.

How did Jesus deal with Satan when tempted in the desert? Jesus struck back with Scripture each time. We need to know what God says in His Word so that we are prepared to fight the enemy, because he is roaring and ready to fight those who are walking with Jesus. Oh yes, opposition comes. But sister, you are on the victorious side. Keep walking. Keep reading. Keep fighting. Our God is faithful.

How are you doing with wielding your sword? Do you need to brush up with some practice?

Miraculously, the Israelites finished the wall in 52 days—a feat beyond any proportion. God was with them. They were committed to prayer; they were committed to their task. They were prepared to do the work and battle the opposition. And they knew they had a big God. They had faith. Doesn't the journey ahead seem a little more manageable when we compare the greatness of our God to our problem? He can do anything! He is powerful, and He is loving. I'm so thankful.

See you in this week's video!

A heart for journey isn't surprised by opposition but knows to handle it with prayer, perspective, and the Word of God.

WATCH THE WEEK 2 VIDEO

Moving Forward

Scriptures in this Session: 2 Peter 3:17–18, Colossians 2:6–7

Also mentioned: Ephesians 4:15, Hebrews 6:1, Colossians 1:9, Matthew 6, Psalm 51:15

Great growth comes on our journeys when we:

1. Have the _____ of a _____.

2. Seek to grow _____ or _____ all situations.

3. Develop a dynamic _____ life.

4. Recognize _____ will vs. _____ will.

5. Live in spiritual _____.

Video lessons are available at KristenTiber.com/AHeartForJourneyVideos.

Week Three

Together

"They devoted themselves to the apostles' teaching and to fellowship, to the breaking of bread and to prayer."

Acts 2:42

Day One

When I was twenty-two, having finished college and back in my hometown, I joined a Bible study at my church. The group consisted of twelve women—each at different places in their journey, but all seeking to grow closer to the Lord. They were hungry to know Him and to know His Word. But what was interesting (and wonderful) about this group of ladies, was the diversity of age. I was the youngest by twenty years. The other women ranged in age from forty-two to sixty-two years old.

I was part of this group for about eight years, meeting every Tuesday night, September to June. I had the pleasure, delight, and blessing of sitting with these women for those years, just learning from them. Watching them. Praying with them. I would hear their heartaches and their joys. I would hear about their marriages and their children, and see how God was moving in the midst of different situations.

They involved me in their lives, and likewise, I shared my life with them. They were with me through job decisions and when I met and married Dan. In fact, I have a picture of all of us together at our wedding. This special group of women shared in my joy as I had my first child and reveled in the excitement of that new journey. I have such precious memories of that time because they were my mentors. We were doing life together and growing in the Lord together.

Turn to Ecclesiastes 4:9–12. What does Solomon say is better than one and why?

The book of Ecclesiastes is a discourse on the meaning of life. It is Solomon's journey of thought on topics like purpose, values, truth, and struggle. After everything Solomon had done and acquired in his life, he spent twelve chapters in Ecclesiastes talking about what is meaningless. Honestly, it is a little bit of a downer for many sections. But the conclusion Solomon arrived at is to fear God and keep His commands (Eccles. 12:13). And so it is against this background that we see Solomon share this wisdom about two being better than one.

The wise king gives us several examples to demonstrate his point. He proposes that two have a good return for their labor. Isn't it nice when we have someone to work with us? For as long as I can remember, my mom has said she would enjoy doing yard work more if someone would just come and sit out in the yard with her. He or she doesn't even have to work; she would just enjoy the company and be motivated to get more done. Solomon takes it further and shows that two working are much more productive and have greater results.

Next, he mentions that if one falls down, the other can help him up. People in our lives can offer great kindness and support—whether physical, emotional, or even spiritual. Being able to help one another and meet needs is beneficial to both parties. Solomon then shares that two can keep each other warm. With Israel's cold winter nights,[34] two could share comfort in this way. His fourth point is that two can help defend each other if attacked. Isn't it nice to feel like you have an ally in tough situations? But Solomon's final thought in this passage switches things up. "A cord of three strands is not quickly broken" (Ecc. 4:12).

What is this cord of three strands? I've often wondered, *Hey, we're talking about two here. How did we get to three?* Here are a few thoughts. We know that three strands make any cord stronger. Some point to this as a reference to the Trinity—the Father, Son, and Holy Spirit. Others reason that Solomon is simply stating that while two are good, three are better. Many have used this verse to relate to a marriage relationship or a friendship, pointing to God as the third-party. And while I'm not sure exegetically if that was the intention, there is no reason we can't consider how two are good but three are better—and if that third is the Lord, now we're talking! Any relationship with Him as the foundation, the common ground, and the interwoven focus will be—without a doubt—stronger.

> ✽**Do you have a relationship where the Lord is the third strand? How is it different than other relationships?**

Look at Genesis 2:18–24. What did God say was not good for Adam?

Human beings were not made to be alone. Whether we are talking the marriage relationship or simply friendships, we were built for community. On this journey of life, we need other people and they need us. Even just among women, we can see that we are wired for meaningful connection.

A friend and I often carpool our kids around. It all began when Anna and my friend's youngest daughter were in kindergarten. We would carpool for school pick-up, then stand in each other's driveway for a while afterward, getting to know each other. These days, we carpool for sports practice, youth group, or simply times of "hanging out" (because big kids don't have play dates!). Our kids know we are pretty incapable of keeping the conversation short, so they usually disappear, and what was meant to be just a few minutes has often turned into an hour or more of chatting, catching up, and sharing life together. Yeah, the kids think we're hilarious.

Let's turn and look at Jesus and His disciples. Did Jesus just teach and instruct all the time or was He relational as well? I'd like you to take notice of a little word with big meaning.

Turn to Mark 3:13–14. Fill in the blank: "He appointed twelve that they might be _____ him . . ."

Jesus didn't merely travel alone and teach. He didn't isolate Himself. He could have done everything alone, but He didn't. He intentionally developed community. Sure, He went off on His own at times to pray and be alone (and don't we all need that?). But day in and day out, Jesus built community. He wanted others along with Him. He spent time with His disciples and even more with His inner circle. Jesus had the twelve disciples, but there was also an inner circle into whom he poured even more. Three disciples. Peter, James, and John were the three men who accompanied Jesus on the mount of transfiguration, who witnessed Jesus raising Jairus' daughter from the dead, and who went further with Jesus into the Garden of Gethsemane than the others.[35] The way Jesus spent time with people is an example for us.

Read what Dr. James Merritt had to say about the importance of community following Jesus' example.

> The way that Jesus chose to live His life on earth is a model for all Christians who have come after Him. As followers of Jesus Christ, we need real fellowship with other believers. We need the kind of fellowship that cannot take place in a worship service on Sunday morning, but rather the kind that happens by living life alongside one another and sharing joys and burdens, sorrows and disappointments, and victories and defeats. We need an inner circle, just like Jesus had. These trusted friends will allow us to be transparent with our sin struggles and will love us enough to be there, yet still hold us accountable to the truth of God's Word. This is biblical community.[36]

Yet another reason to nest at church and be rooted in your local body of believers! A biblical church can support, encourage, and challenge you. But it doesn't just happen on Sunday mornings, it comes with getting involved. There shouldn't be any lone Christians.

Now, I certainly know that there are individuals who are unable to worship at church because of health issues or disabilities. And if this is you, I hope that your church comes to *you*. We had a lady at church who went home to be with the Lord this past year. She had been homebound for at least the last three years of her life. She was a widow for many years prior—in fact, I never knew her

A heart for journey recognizes the importance of community.

husband. But she had been faithful at church, and we loved her. People from our congregation were so very supportive and loving to her with frequent visits, spending time listening to her fascinating stories, and my favorite, on a few Sunday evenings each summer, the church took worship to her house. We all sat in her front yard, with her tucked in the threshold of her front door. Most of the time was spent with her holding a tissue to her face and boy, it was hard to not cry right along with her. And although, I am sure she felt alone at times, I also know she felt loved by her church.

Community goes both ways. It is not just for our benefit but also for others. What a good reminder for us to look for those in need of community or simply those in search of a friend.

> *"Rejoice with those who rejoice; mourn with those who mourn. Live in harmony with one another. Do not be proud, but be willing to associate with people of low position. Do not be conceited."*
>
> —ROMANS 12:15–16

✣**Read Romans 12:15–16 in the margin. What does this verse tell us about the heart of community?**

Do you have a community? People with whom you can rejoice *and* weep; people who will love and support you, and you with them? Do you have friends at church or elsewhere who will be part of your cord? If not, let's ask the Lord right now to begin to develop a community with whom you can walk on this journey of life. You aren't meant to do this alone. A community can provide help, support, comfort, protection, and strength.

Who is your community? Do you find yourself in need of one?

And please allow me to say this, if you are really struggling with developing a community, it may be that you need to build greater intimacy with the Lord first. I remember someone once mentioning a "famine of friends." If God has you in this kind of season, it may be first and foremost that He wants to draw you closer to Him in a new way.

Also remember this is a journey and communities can change over time. Friends may come in and out of your life. You still have new people to meet and new relationships to build. Who knows where God is going to take you and who you'll meet along the road?

I thank God for the way He used those Bible study women in my life and the countless individuals He has surrounded me with since. We were made for community and for fellowship with each other.

Tomorrow, we will look at a young woman who made a choice that led to blessing and new community after a period of great personal loss. Her story is a familiar one, but I'm praying we see it with fresh eyes.

Day Two

Who is in your circle of community? The other day, Dan and I were talking about the different circles in which we live. We have church, family, work, homeschool, college, and neighbors. He can add volleyball and basketball communities to the mix as well. There are many circles within which we all live. Different seasons yield different circles. But have you noticed how the Lord brings different people into our lives for different purposes—to fill voids, to satisfy needs, and to help us grow closer to Him?

I have a friend who lost her dad when she was very young. As a child, she had prayed for a new dad—one that would be everything hoped for in a father. When she married, she received all of that and more in her new father-in-law. To hear my friend talk about him, is to want to love this dad as well. The Lord gave her a father. It wasn't in the timing she had asked for as a child, but she

"And let us consider how we may spur one another on toward love and good deeds, not giving up meeting together, as some are in the habit of doing, but encouraging one another—and all the more as you see the Day approaching."

—HEBREWS 10:24–25

would tell you that this man was worth the wait. He was the best father-in-law, and God used this man to meet the desire of my friend's heart.

Today, we are going to look at a woman from Moab who married an Israelite but lost her husband after ten years of marriage. And instead of going back to her own family, she clung to her mother-in-law and traveled with her to Israel. This young widow left her homeland, a land filled with idolatry and pagan gods, and journeyed with her beloved mother-in-law to a less-than-promising future. In this new land as a foreigner, she would likely never marry. She would probably live in poverty her entire life. But that didn't happen. Instead, God established her in a beautiful community of faith. Into great tragedy and pain, God brought joy, beauty, and transformation. He gave this woman a new love story, a marriage to a man of great character and kindness, and her first child who would become the great-grandfather of David and be listed in the genealogy of the Messiah, Jesus.

Turn to the book of Ruth. Let's read Ruth 1:1–5. What took Elimelech's family away from Bethlehem, Judah (in the promised land) to a foreign country? What happened to this man and his family while there?

> "... for it is God who works in you, both to will and to work for his good pleasure."
>
> —PHILIPPIANS 2:13 ESV

The book of Ruth is a short book of only four chapters, but where it lacks in length, it is rich with detail. Truly, we could spend an entire study on this little book! It is an account of loss and redemption, and of disadvantage and restoration. It is a story of heartache and hard seasons transformed into the beauty of family and community. It tells of commitment and blessing, and of a God who is faithfully working all things out according to His good pleasure (Phil. 2:13). I'm sure we can all find ourselves in there somewhere!

The book is set in the time of the judges, an era known for great disobedience and men doing what was right in their own eyes (Judg. 17:6). God used the judges to call His people back to Himself. The famine, that had Elimelech running fifty miles out of Bethlehem to Moab,[37] was the judgement of God, as was every other famine mentioned in the Bible.[38] Ironically, the name of Elimelech's hometown means "house of bread," and yet that is precisely what it lacked.

Read Ruth 1:6–18. What did Naomi instruct her daughters-in-law to do? What did each young woman decide?

Can you hear their weeping? How heartbroken these three women must have been to consider leaving each other. In the midst of mourning the deaths of their husbands, they at least had one another. God had given them that. But after Naomi instructed the girls to go home, and they both initially refused, she started explaining that they would do better to find husbands among their own people. Naomi was too old to bear more children, let alone find a husband and produce sons the women would have to wait for to grow up. But Ruth persisted. She would not leave Naomi. Instead, she left the familiar fields of Moab to travel to Israel, a land whose people were not supposed to marry individuals from pagan nations lest they were led into idolatry themselves.

In the famous verses of 16–17, Ruth poetically and beautifully stood her ground and expressed her deep commitment to stay with Naomi. Where Naomi would go, she would go. Naomi's people would become Ruth's people. Naomi's God, her God. Wouldn't you love to sit with these two on the porch and chat? Not only would I love to see their relationship at work, but I would also love to ask Ruth about claiming the Hebrew God as her own.

Ruth was a Moabitess. Moabites worshipped many gods, but their primary god was Chemosh.[39] On behalf of this false god, the people offered human sacrifices and committed many immoral acts.[40] Ruth put all that aside and chose Naomi's God as her God.

Please understand that had Ruth gone back to her family, she would have had the chance to marry again. But by going home with Naomi, her chances were limited. In that time, without a male head of the household and the security a husband or son provided, a life of poverty was likely. And yet, Ruth pressed on. I think Ruth needed Naomi as much as we will see that Naomi needed Ruth. And what a blessing Ruth will prove to be to her mother-in-law later in the account.

So Naomi and Ruth returned to Bethlehem, but after experiencing such great loss, Naomi decided to change her name. Read Ruth 1:19–22 and record Naomi's new name and meaning.

Naomi blamed God for everything that happened in Moab. Commentators agree that she incorrectly removed all human responsibility from the happenings. After all, they were the ones who chose to leave the promised land. But people handle loss differently. Many of us have gone through situations of great loss. Things that change us. Naomi was so impacted (and who wouldn't be) by her loss that upon returning to Bethlehem, when the women asked if this was Naomi returned home, she told them to call her Mara because of her bitterness. This was a woman who left Israel full, but returned empty—physically and spiritually.

Have you experienced times of emptiness? What were they prompted by?

Despite the fact that Naomi felt empty, she still had Ruth with her. Who are the people who have stood by you in the hardest of situations? God put them there for a purpose. How did the Lord use them in your life?

It is sometimes in the most challenging of situations that we have the opportunity to see God work mightily. Sometimes He moves in big and obvious ways. And at other times, God moves marvelously through the happenstances and "it just so happened . . ." of His providence. Things are about to change for Naomi and Ruth. Why? Because of God's graciousness to a bitter woman and a devoted foreigner.

✢**Read Ruth 2:1–8. In whose field did Ruth happen to be gleaning?**

When Ruth and her mother-in-law returned to Naomi's hometown of Bethlehem in Judah, the barley harvest was beginning. Ruth asked Naomi if she could go to the fields and glean behind the harvesters. Gleaning was something the poor were able to do in the fields after the workers passed through. God had instructed his people to leave behind some of the crop so that the poor could gather what was left and find sustenance (Lev. 19:9–10, 23:22).

Now there is key wording that I would like us to pay particular attention to, and it is found in Ruth 2:3. Some versions convey that Ruth "happened to come" to Boaz's field, while others say, "As it turned out . . . ." And oh, how I love this! When Ruth stepped foot onto Boaz's field, it was no accident! It was divinely arranged by the Lord. Sometimes God allows us to go down roads that are hard. But when He does this, you can count on the fact that not only is a harvest coming, but also that God will arrange and orchestrate events in our lives for our good and His glory. And at some point, we will look back and see His hand at work and His sovereignty at play.

> One of the glorious things, as we go through this world today, is to know that our times are in His hands; to know that He is ordering the events of this universe; and to know that God has said nothing can come to a child of His without His permission. You must remember that there was a hedge around Job, and even Satan couldn't touch him until God gave permission. God will not give permission unless it serves some lofty and worthy purpose. —J. Vernon McGee[41]

✢ **Have you witnessed coincidences that turned out to be so much more—times you realized God was at work? Share the details below.**

> A heart for journey sees the happenstances of life as the happenings of a sovereign God.

As Ruth continued to live with Naomi and work in Boaz's fields, her kindness to her mother-in-law was noticed by Boaz. He showed Ruth benevolence and favor—speaking blessings over her and offering protection and provision in his fields. And Naomi (who was probably starting to hope once again) recognized God's providence in the happenstance of the field in which Ruth was working. Under Naomi's instruction, Ruth made a request to Boaz to marry her and fulfill his role as kinsman redeemer.

A kinsman redeemer was someone who would help a relative out of a difficult situation.[42] According to Levirate law, if a man died, his brother (or a close relative) was to marry his childless wife and buy the estate (if it had been sold), thereby preserving the family line of the deceased and providing for the widow. Other duties of a kinsman redeemer included avenging the death of a relative who had been murdered, buying a family member who had been sold into slavery, and providing for relatives in need.[43]

What I find very interesting and a confirmation of Ruth's faith in the Hebrew God, is that Boaz without hesitation considered the marriage, and the town elders offered no dispute. Ruth was not a Jew by birth, but by confession. But she had likely started following Jewish law, and we know that she had established a good reputation in Bethlehem and was taking refuge under the God of Israel (Ruth 2:11–12). Boaz was not marrying a pagan worshiper; he was marrying Ruth, follower of the one true God.

In the last chapter of the book, Boaz married Ruth (after a closer relative passed as the kinsman redeemer). Boaz bought back the estate of Elimelech, and the couple had a son. Please don't miss the fact that Ruth was unable to conceive with her first husband for ten years. However now, in a literal rendering of

Ruth 4:13 "the LORD gave her [Ruth] conception."⁴⁴ God richly blessed Ruth, giving her more people to love and with whom to share her life.

Even from Naomi's perspective, God did a great work of restoration. In Ruth 4:15, the women of the town told Naomi that having Ruth as a daughter-in-law was better than seven sons, which Israelites considered to be the ideal family.⁴⁵ But here, Ruth was better! And the contrast between Naomi's emptiness upon leaving Moab and her fullness at the end of the book—with a sweet grandchild being laid in her lap—is poignant. Before, she had no security. Now, she had family. Upon her return to Israel, she had no prospects of a pleasant life, but now she had fullness and joy. Even the town women called her Naomi at the end of the book. I wonder if Naomi changed her mind or the women just knew by the smile on her face. Our God is good. He is a God of restoration and redemption.

✢**In your own life, have you seen God bring blessing after hardship?**

Do you see any similarities between Boaz and Jesus? Both are kinsman redeemers. Both bought something back and redeemed it. For Boaz, it was Ruth, Naomi, and Elimelech's estate. But for Jesus, it was us. He bought our freedom from sin and rescued us from death. As one commentator notes, "There can be no redemption without the paying of a price."⁴⁶ But it wasn't with money that Jesus paid our redemption, it was with His blood. And what's more, we who were outsiders and foreigners are now brought into God's family through our kinsman redeemer, Jesus. He bought us back and gave us this incredible community of faith in which to live and grow. A place of belonging. Thank you, Lord!

> "You turned my wailing into dancing; you removed my sackcloth and clothed me with joy, that my heart may sing your praises and not be silent. LORD my God, I will praise you forever."
>
> —PSALM 30:11–12

Day Three

In our study this week, we have seen the importance of community and how God brings people into our lives for specific purposes. He is able to bring His children into community even after life feels like it will forever be bitter. Like Naomi and Ruth, we need other people on our journeys. We are not meant to do this life alone.

So if we know God's design is to be in community, *how* do we build it? What are some things we can do? How do we keep our eyes open for people to invite into our circles? Let's get into Scripture and see.

When we think about community in the Word, one of the most stunning examples to consider is the early Jerusalem church.

> ✢**Turn to Acts 2:42–47. List everything the believers did in these verses.**

"Togetherness is one of the most important themes in the New Testament."

—*Got Questions*[47]

In Acts 2, Luke gives us a beautiful picture of the community life experienced by the early church. It is an ideal picture and a great model for us as we seek to engage with those whom God will use on our journeys and vice versa.

Let's take a look at the first four things listed that the believers did and discover the principles for our own lives:

> They devoted themselves to the apostles' _____. As believers, we are never finished growing and learning. We need to be sitting under biblical teaching and preaching.
>
> They were devoted to _____. This word in the Greek is *koinonia* and it refers to having something in common.[48] Fellowship is what happens when people with a common interest (here it is their

common faith in Jesus Christ) come together and spend time with each other. It is a safe place to share, grow, encourage, and challenge.

They were devoted to the breaking of _____. Many commentators believe this "breaking of bread" was more than a common meal; it was the observance of the Lord's supper.[49] The believers were remembering what Jesus did for them on the cross, as commanded by the Lord Himself at the last supper. We will see later that they also shared common meals together in their homes.

They were devoted to _____. This is important on multiple fronts. First, we know that prayer is effective (James 5:16). It works! God hears our prayers and answers. Second, group prayer connects our hearts with others because it allows for the opportunity to see into the hearts of those with whom we pray. It can be a very special thing. You may not feel comfortable praying aloud with others, but if I could encourage you on this, it is a great blessing to gather and pray together. Prayer is simply you and your brothers and sisters talking to your Heavenly Father. And you don't have to start with big, lofty prayers. If nothing else, simply focus on praising God for one thing and bring a request before Him.

Following these initial four activities, Luke tells us that the believers were filled with awe at the miracles performed by the apostles (verse 43). Was this an awe for the apostles themselves? No, the glory didn't fall to them. The believers were joined together in an awe for God and how He was moving.

Next in verse 44, we see that all the believers were _____ and had everything in _____.

This is building relationships through time. Time together builds relationships, fellowship, and community. You may have also noticed in our passage that the believers voluntarily and generously gave to others. They helped those in need.

"For where two or three are gathered together in My name, I am there in the midst of them."

—MATTHEW 18:20
NKJV

When people share experiences, it bonds them together. Add service to it and the results are even greater!

When Dan and I used to lead the youth group at our church, one of our favorite things to do was take the teens on trips—especially mission trips—because the time allowed for such great bonding. One year, we went to Salem Ranch, a Christian "last chance" horse farm in Illinois. The ranch was basically a boy's last opportunity for reform before going to juvenile detention. It was most certainly a place out of our kids' comfort zones and many of the residents came from diverse and rough backgrounds. We spent the days doing yard work, painting, and more. Our evenings were spent playing crazy youth group games with our kids and the boys (the messy games were my favorite) and having the opportunity to lead in devotions.

We have wonderful memories from that trip. Memories of kids working hard and trying new things. Girls up on ladders painting a teacher's apartment bathroom. Boys sleeping on a gym floor with fans and way too much Axe cologne. I remember two of our kids sitting silently in front of an oven to catch (by hand) a family of mice who had made a home in the stove so that we could bake lasagna for dinner. (This cabin wasn't regularly used; in fact, we were cleaning and painting it for future use.)

The entire experience of serving others, sharing the love of Christ, getting to know the staff, and being together was community-building for our youth group. The week of shared goals and missions, long car rides, and late-night discussions—it was all time together and it was great!

> **What is an act of service you can collectively do with friends, neighbors, your church family, or others? And how might this not only bless others, but also benefit the group?**

Another activity we see the believers doing in Acts 2 is the sharing of meals in their homes. Not only were smaller groups of individuals meeting together and getting to know each other, but they were also sharing food together. Food is amazing like that, isn't it? I don't know what it is, but eating together is great for building community. Church potlucks, family dinners, parties . . . Maybe it is the conversations that take place, the sharing of lives over a meal, or the fact that people may feel more at ease with something in their hands to hold. Yes, food can help with something like that.

When Peter was in second grade, he was given a technology survey to assess what the students already knew and what they hoped to learn. Peter knew basic computer skills, and he wanted to learn to type fast. The last question though on the survey asked, "What is something that you would like to do in Technology Class?" My kid's answer? "Have snacks when done." He is completely his father's son. But yes, Peter, food makes it all better.

Do you have people over to your home for meals? This is an area in which I would like to grow—not because our hearts are against it, but simply because of time and schedules. When my mother-in-law was living, we had Sunday dinners (actually a lunchtime meal for those of you who aren't accustomed to the terminology and honestly, I'm still confused by it). All of Dan's siblings and their families, along with whomever else was invited last minute, gathered at their house after church to enjoy a meal together. Was community built? Oh yes, it was.

Where would you like to grow in strengthening and building your community?

Why is community important for your journey?

A large part of community is possessing a genuine interest in the lives of others. Take the time to initiate a conversation and find out what is going on in someone's life. How can you pray for them? How can you be of help? I am often surprised at how taken back people are at a simple willingness to help. What might be very easy for you may mean so much to someone else. Take the time to get to know people. Be a blessing. Make them feel valued because they are created by God in His image and every life is precious.

My husband, Dan, is amazing at community. He can create community wherever he goes. Whatever line we are standing in, there is my husband trying to start up a conversation. It is something I love about him, unless we are trying to hurry somewhere!

A couple of years ago on a trip to Disney World, he and I split to go on different rides. I took the kids to Toy Story Mania and he wanted to get on Rockin' Roller Coaster before our trip came to an end. I texted him when we got off only to find out that he was now in line for another rollercoaster. When we met up, I asked if he minded riding alone. He said, "Oh no, I wasn't alone. I started talking with a guy on the first ride, and so we went and did the second one together. His wife works at Disney and I got the inside information on rides and food." And all I could think was, *Of course, he did*. That is Dan. Yes, it takes a while to leave anywhere when he is talking, but he is so good at building community and making people feel valued.

Let's take a moment and look at building intentional community outside of your church. This is a great opportunity for outreach. Every year, Dan and I host a neighborhood gathering. Over the years, we have had ice cream socials, donut and cider parties, and this year, we switched it up and had a nacho party with more toppings than any normal person could have wanted to put on chips and nacho cheese. We always have a great turnout, and people surprise me with how genuinely appreciative they are that we host this. We are very thankful for our neighborhood and those who live here. We want to be intentional about building relationships, being available to help others, and developing community with our neighbors. Our hope in everything we do is ultimately to bring glory to God. But we also want our lives to point to Christ and we pray for open doors to share our faith. We want to see the lost anywhere and everywhere come to Jesus for the hope and restoration we ourselves have experienced.

> ✢**What are things you could do to tangibly share God's love with those around you?**

> **Is there a group outside of your church with whom you would like to build community? How might you start or continue?**

> **What does Scripture tell us about the believers' community in Acts 2:47?**

"Live such good lives among the pagans that, though they accuse you of doing wrong, they may see your good deeds and glorify God on the day he visits us."

—1 PETER 2:12

How beautiful! Communities of faith aren't meant to be exclusive clubs. They are meant to be open doors where people are saved, disciples are made, and we all grow to look more like Jesus. The believers' community was built with teaching, fellowship, prayer, time together, meals, and service. Grab the extra chairs. More friends are coming!

Day Four

I was in my office last week while the kids were eating lunch. Usually we eat together, but I had a couple of things I had to get done, so they were on their own for the day. From behind the closed door of my office though, I could tell there was more than the usual commotion going on. I heard Peter (obviously with food in his mouth) say to his sister, "You know, Anna, there's a rule in the Bible about not murdering or killing someone, but there's not a rule about spitting your carrots in someone's face."

This is a funny little example, but it proves a point. No matter how wonderful your community is, doing life with others can still be messy. Relationships can be complex. Why? Because we are all sinful human beings, and we all still have more growing up to do in Christ. Very likely, there will be times throughout your life when you want to drop out, fight back, or even spit carrots in someone's face, but that is not what God wants for you. We are not meant to be lone ranger Christians. We are meant to live in unity (with grace and truth). We are meant to treat others as we would like to be treated. Yes, there may be times when you feel that it would be easier to disengage, but press through, because we were not made to be alone. And many of life's greatest blessings and joys can come through others.

> Please know that I am speaking of typical conflict and relational messes. This is not meant to address abusive or immoral situations.

How do we handle those times when people are annoying or when there is disagreement or strife? Do we disconnect? Do we check out and just keep to ourselves? Now, I am not talking about an unhealthy relationship that needs boundaries. I'm talking about doing life together and how it isn't always a bed of roses. Sometimes it can get pretty thorny. How do we handle those instances?

Turn once again to Romans 12:15–16. What are Paul's instructions?

Once there was a group of people whom I dearly valued and loved, but there came a day when I stood alone—I expected one behavior from the group, but instead I was met with the opposite. We greatly differed on where we stood on a matter. To be completely open, first of all, I was shocked. I didn't expect the difference in our thinking. And I sat there feeling disillusioned, disappointed, as well as a little angry that this was what it had come to. And as quickly as I was feeling a flood of emotions, the Spirit of God spoke to my heart and said, "Serve them."

He didn't say, "Go ahead, be angry." Nor did He say, "Oh child, you're right." He simply said, "Serve them," and it was like a holy hush filled my mind. I had wanted to be angry and think *all* the thoughts, but the Lord was telling me to put that aside and instead, humble myself. My eyes filled up with tears and I had a choice in front of me. The Lord was clear on how He wanted me to respond. So I made a point over those next weeks to do things that served this group. I sent a card to encourage someone, a few texts, as well as other things. And God changed my heart in the process. No, we never did agree on everything, but that wasn't my purpose. I was supposed to stay humble and serve.

This has often made me wonder if some of our relational conflicts could be better approached, handled, and resolved if we were able to come to every situation with a humble heart. Humility is tough! We *want* to assert our rights. We *want* to be strong, and we *want* to be right. But what if on those hard issues (without compromising truth), we could approach the situation in humility? Would that make things go better?

This is something I am still working on. How about you? To what extent are you able to maintain humility in the midst of conflict with others?

✣Let's look at a great example. Read Philippians 2:5–11. Who are we talking about, and how did He humble Himself?

Here is someone who had all the power of the universe, and yet He humbled Himself. Jesus did not assert His right on so many occasions when He could have. He remained silent when questioned by the high priest (a man who was supposed to be serving God and watching for the coming Messiah). Jesus laid His glory and majesty aside for a greater purpose. He is the ultimate example of strength and humility.

The question we have to ask is: what is our goal in the midst of conflict? Our goal is to bring glory to God, to point people to Christ, and to build up not tear down relationships. We can most definitely stand up for ourselves without pushing others to the ground or hastily giving up on people. How are we doing on that?

Let's do a theme study on humility. Have you done a word or theme study before? It is a great practice when you want to see more about the importance of or the biblical teaching on a particular concept. Search the word "humility" (or "humble") in the back of your Bible or in an online concordance such as Bible Gateway, Blue Letter Bible, or Bible Hub. Then start working through the verses. Today, you may do your own personal study or you can use the verses I've listed for you below. Take a look at what each verse is saying about humility and jot down a few notes.

2 Chronicles 34:27

Proverbs 16:18

Isaiah 57:15

> *"For even the Son of Man came not to be served but to serve, and to give his life as a ransom for many."*
>
> —MARK 10:45 ESV

> *"If my people, who are called by my name, will humble themselves and pray and seek my face and turn from their wicked ways, then I will hear from heaven, and I will forgive their sin and will heal their land."*
>
> —2 CHRONICLES 7:14

Week Three

Zephaniah 2:3

Matthew 23:10–12

Galatians 2:20

Philippians 2:3–4

1 Peter 5:5–6

What are your thoughts after seeing these verses on humility? How does this change how we might approach others we meet along the way in our journeys?

✢**Write down any thoughts you have on humility after looking at these verses.**

"Now I, Nebuchadnezzar, praise and exalt and glorify the King of heaven, because everything he does is right and all his ways are just. And those who walk in pride he is able to humble."

—DANIEL 4:37

A Heart for Journey

A heart for journey seeks to walk in humility before God and others.

Walking with others in community isn't always perfect. We must tend to our own attitude and heart in times of conflict. Stay in check. Remember, people are at different places on their journey. Walk with grace, love, and humility.

Day Five

There is one more thing I would like to share with you about walking with others on our journeys. And this is something we see several times in the Scriptures. Ready to dig in today?

> **✢Turn to Acts 16:1–3. Who does Paul meet on this second missionary journey? What did Paul want to do according to verse 3a?**

This begins a wonderful relationship that is seen throughout Paul's epistles. As Paul and Timothy traveled and got to know each other, Paul thought very highly and lovingly about this young man. In fact, of the thirteen books of the New Testament that Paul wrote, Timothy is mentioned in ten of them and listed as a co-author for six of the letters.

> **Look at both 1 Corinthians 4:17 and Philippians 2:22. What did Paul call Timothy even though they were not related? Jot down what they did together.**

Now Paul also refers to Timothy as a brother and co-worker in the faith, but at the heart of their relationship was a nurturing, encouraging, and challenging push of discipleship and mentoring. Paul mentored Timothy, and they spent much time together. As Timothy grew, Paul sent him out to work for the Gospel on several occasions. When Paul was in Macedonia, he told Timothy to stay in Ephesus (a place Paul had previously spent much time) with the expressed purpose of correcting doctrinal errors and false teaching. Later in the years of their relationship, Paul wrote two letters to Timothy that we have in the New Testament, and those letters are filled with words of encouragement, instruction, and accountability.

Why are we looking at these two men in Scripture? Because being on a journey means walking with other believers, but not just ones who are at the same place in life as us. We are called to train future generations to walk faithfully with the Lord on their own path—directing them to the Scriptures, encouraging them to be faithful, and helping them to walk with purpose, love, and hope.

Let's turn to Titus 2:3–5. What kind of mentoring relationships do you find here?

God has given us one another within the church to build up and encourage, to train and teach, to love and share life. This passage in Titus 2 can be boiled down to three things: love, relationships, and conduct.[50] Now I don't think Paul meant by any means that this is all there is, but look how good these concepts are. Love: love for our families, patterned after the way that Jesus loves.[51] Relationships: building good, healthy relationships with those around us (including husbands and children). Conduct: making sure that our lives match our beliefs.

Remember that Bible study group I was in after college that I mentioned in day one of this week? That was Titus 2 in action! This was the method Paul shared here—the older training the younger women. And isn't it wonderful that age is not defined? The nature of the relationship is that there is a younger woman and a woman who is older than her.

Susan Hunt, author of a mentoring book called *Spiritual Mothering*, gave this definition for mentoring: "When a woman possessing faith and spiritual

"It is interesting that of all the ways Paul could have told the women to combat the decadence of their culture, he told them to invest their energies in training the younger women to live Christianly in their society."

—Susan Hunt[52]

maturity enters into a nurturing relationship with a younger woman in order to encourage and equip her to live for God's glory."

How wonderful this is! Nurturing relationships to encourage and equip all to the glory of God. Isn't that our goal on this journey as well? To live for God's glory? I mentor a young woman, and here is my prayer for her: that she would continue to grow stronger in her faith, finding her strength in the Lord, following Him whole-heartedly, fulfilling His purpose and plans for her life, while being encouraged and equipped to live for Him and His glory.

> ✣**Do you have a Timothy? I know there are plenty out there who need the support of a fellow sister in Christ. Are you open to the idea?**

> A heart for journey intentionally serves future generations by helping younger believers grow in their faith.

One thing I seem to hear frequently is that women feel inadequate to mentor someone else. And I've heard this from women whom I would love to be mentored by. Again from Susan Hunt, "If you are a Christian woman who is seeking to grow in the faith and to live obediently, then you are qualified for spiritual motherhood."[53] Being a mentor doesn't mean you are a perfect woman, but it does mean that you are seeking to please the Lord and serve Him.

At the women's mentoring event that starts off a new cycle of mentoring at our church, I take a moment to address this. Many mentors feel intimidated when asked to take on this task. You may be initially feeling the same way about the idea. But let me remind you that mentoring is walking *alongside* one another. It is growing *together*. When you're a mentor, it is usually not because you are exceedingly confident in your abilities, but rather it is because you believe that God can take what you have to offer and do something incredible. Mentors don't have all the answers, and they are not shy about saying that, but what they will do is point others to Jesus. They will walk alongside the younger women in their season of life. They will encourage, challenge, and grow with them. Then hopefully one day down the road, the young woman becomes the older woman to someone else. And in this way, faithful living and encouragement is perpetuated in the family of God.

Now, I would be utterly remiss if I didn't turn the tables for just a moment and ask who your Paul is as well? We all need a Timothy *and* a Paul—someone we are helping to grow in faith and someone who is helping us to grow as well.

Do you have a Paul, or have you had different mentors throughout your life? List them here and share what you learned from them.

> We all need a Timothy and a Paul—someone we are helping to grow in faith and someone who is helping us to grow as well.

When I think of the women reading this book in their family room with their Bible in hand or the ladies gathered in churches participating in this study together, I see magnificent treasures. Treasures of experiences, of a variety of life situations, of walking through tough times with faith. I also see a God who has been faithful and who has given us each other. Yes, this is our own journey, but we are not meant to do it alone. God has graciously given us other believers to grow with and love, including those future generations who will walk the road of faith with grace, courage, and their own heart for journey.

> If you would like more information about starting a mentoring ministry at your church, go to www.KristenTiber.com/blog/mentoringministry.

WATCH THE WEEK 3 VIDEO

The Gracious God

Scriptures in this Session: 1 Kings 17–19, Hebrews 4:14–16

Elijah learned that his gracious God is _____, sustainer, and _____ over all creation.

On our journey, we are either _____ God or we are _____ something else—the false, fake or temporary.

Just as Elijah prayed to "the God of Abraham, Isaac, and Jacob," our faith will be bolstered as we remember that our God has a history of _____ _____.

Our High Priest, Jesus, understands what we _____ and how we _____—and He never leaves us.

When we feel alone, God will _____ _____, and we can find encouragement and hope in His kindness, sovereignty, and faithfulness.

How gracious is our God!

Video lessons are available at KristenTiber.com/AHeartForJourneyVideos.

Week Four

A Heart to Serve

*"For whoever wants to save their life will lose it,
but whoever loses their life for me and for the gospel will save it.
What good is it for someone to gain the whole world,
yet forfeit their soul?"*

Mark 8: 35–36

Day One

A few years ago, we were driving to church on a Sunday morning. We were nearly halfway there when I looked down at my feet and noticed that I had forgotten to take off my indoor Crocs flip flops and put on dress shoes. I gasped, pulled my foot off the gas pedal, and shared my dilemma with Dan and the kids. There was no way I could walk into church with nice clothes on my body and Crocs on my feet. So, we turned around. As I expressed my thought, "I can't believe I did that," Dan shared that he saw the shoes but didn't say anything.

"Why not?" I exclaimed.

He replied, "Not my problem."

"*What?*" I shot back as the conversation picked up speed like my minivan.

He began to get defensive and tried to reconcile his comment as meaning it wasn't his concern or his fault—or some other foolishness like that. But the phrase, "Not my problem," would now enter our family dialogue in comical infamy.

Upon our arrival at church with the proper shoes, I rushed down the hall in order to get to our Sunday School class before Dan. The high schoolers were all there since we were running a few minutes late. I quickly explained what happened and asked that when Dan made his first request during class, that they look at him and respond in unison, "Not my problem."

They did beautifully. And I felt quite satisfied. But it was nothing compared to what I felt later that afternoon when a certain husband was in the bathroom and shouted out, asking for me to bring him toilet paper. Guess what response he heard?

Well, I can think of another man who thought an *entire city* wasn't his problem. This week, we are going to talk about the importance of serving and radically loving others on this journey of life. We'll read about a prophet who wasn't interested in delivering a message from the Lord to a people He cared about. This prophet lacked compassion, a love for others, and even a solitary, benevolent thought toward the people to whom God was calling him—so much so that he ran in the exact opposite direction.

Read Jonah 1:1–3. What did the Lord instruct Jonah to do? What did he do instead?

Jonah lived during the time of Jeroboam II, king of Israel (the northern kingdom). He is mentioned in 2 Kings 14:25 as prophesying during Jeroboam's rule, which was 793–753 BC.[54] If you'd like to put it into perspective, this is before the northern kingdom was taken into captivity by Assyria in 722 BC.[55] This is the time period of the prophets warning Israel and Judah to return to God.

Jonah, the son of Amittai, was a prophet of the Lord, but not called to prophesy to the Hebrew people alone. God called Jonah to go to the great city of Nineveh and to prophesy against its inhabitants. A prophet often denounced and rebuked other nations, but rarely did one have to visit those lands and share the message face to face.[56]

Nineveh was a leading city of the Assyrian Empire. The lively metropolis sat on the Tigris River about six hundred miles upriver from the Persian Gulf in Iraq.[57] The city of Nineveh and the suburbs had a circumference of eight miles and contained about 600,000 people.[58] Now the Assyrians were not an especially lovely people. In fact, they were quite wicked.

The city was known for sin, idolatry, endless cruelty, and the brutal torture of enemies. Let's just say mercy wasn't in the Assyrian playbook. They impaled victims on sharp poles, beheaded, skinned,[59] and even buried people in the desert up to their heads, putting a thong through their tongues and then letting the hot sun beat down on them. It was said that their victims would go crazy before dying.[60]

Assyria was not friendly toward Israel either. And it is to this people that Jonah was called to prophesy. So instead of starting the journey to Nineveh, Jonah went down to Joppa. Nineveh was five hundred miles northeast of Israel.[61] Joppa was in the complete opposite direction. In fact, the Scriptures specifically tell us that Jonah paid a fare for a ship heading to Tarshish. Commentators differ on where they think Tarshish was. Some think Africa, but many believe it was in Spain—the farthest known geographical point at that time.[62] In Solomon's day, a ship sailing to and from Tarshish would not have returned for three years.[63] How about that for trying to run from God?

✤**Have you ever felt God leading you to do something that you *did not* want to do? If so, how did you respond?**

> A heart for journey is open to being used by God, even when His ways differ from our own.

✤**Why do you think Jonah didn't want to go to Nineveh?**

Jonah made a big deal about not going to Nineveh. Why? I think there are several reasons. But first and foremost, Jonah knew God. He knew God was compassionate and loving (as he will himself confess in chapter four). Jonah knew that if God was calling him to go to Nineveh, God was also ready to extend mercy if the people changed their ways. But Jonah did not want the Ninevites saved. Jonah was an Israelite; Assyria was an enemy. Why would he want God to be merciful to Nineveh? In his mind, they only deserved punishment. Warren Wiersbe points out that "Jonah's narrow patriotism took precedence over his theology."[64] Jonah knew that if God sent him to share the message, God would be willing to spare the city if the Ninevites repented.

Let's take a moment to remind ourselves of who the Israelites were supposed to be in the grand scheme of things. Let's look back to the Abrahamic covenant.

Read Genesis 12:1–3. What were the Jews supposed to be to all people?

Ultimately, the blessing to the whole earth was Jesus, the Messiah, who came out of Israel. But Wiersbe also points out that when the Jews were obedient to God, blessings followed for other nations. Whereas when they were disobedient, trouble followed (such as in the case of Abraham lying about Sarah being his wife).[65] Jonah had forgotten that Israel was to be a blessing to *all* peoples. The prophet acted like God's blessing was for the Hebrews alone.[66] His fists were clenched, and he was not ready to extend the possibility of grace to a people such as the Ninevites.

How about us? Do we live with clenched fists or open hands? Do we see our lives as a means of showing God's kindness, love, and redeeming grace to those with whom we come into contact? We, as new covenant believers, are also meant to be a blessing to others. The Scriptures are full of ways we can do this. Instructions to think and act beyond ourselves come from the lips of Jesus, Paul, and others.

- Be salt to the world (Matt. 5:13).
- Help the weak, hungry, poor, homeless, sick, and imprisoned (Acts 20:35, Matt. 25:34–36).
- Pray for others (1 Tim. 2:1, James 5:16).
- Love others as Jesus has loved us (John 15:12).
- Encourage others, and build them up (1 Thess. 5:11).
- As we have been comforted, comfort others (2 Cor. 1:3–4).
- Show hospitality (Heb. 13:1–2).
- Do good and share (Heb. 13:16).

We are a blessed people because of the riches we have in Christ. We were not meant to be hoarders of God's love, mercy, and grace. But rather, we are called to live an intentional life of outward service. How? We can live with open hands—hands ready to extend kindness and love, to deliberately think of others and their needs, and to generously serve with our money, time, and possessions.

> "Do nothing out of selfish ambition or vain conceit. Rather, in humility value others above yourselves, not looking to your own interests but each of you to the interests of the others."
>
> —PHILIPPIANS 2:3–4

As we spend ourselves on others, not only will we show the love of God, but we will find that we focus less on our own struggles and enjoy the many blessings that a giving heart yields.

Let's look at another way to bless others. In Romans 10, Paul refers back to a verse in the book of Isaiah. Please read Isaiah 52:7 and write it below. Underline any key phrases.

My friend Tara (Aunt Tara to my kids) thinks feet are weird. My kids know this and Peter will affectionately bring up feet as much as he can when we're all together. Yes, feet can be stinky and different looking. They can have odd shapes and sizes, dry skin, and crooked toes. Not many people would think feet are beautiful, but Isaiah does. Isaiah announces how beautiful "are the feet of those who bring good news." There is no greater blessing you can share with a person than to tell him or her the good news of Jesus and what He has done in your life.

We will delve into this more later, but remember: people are lost and hurting. People are broken. People need Jesus more than anything else. The restoration of our spiritual condition is the greatest need we have. It doesn't matter how much money someone has or doesn't have, what political party is leading in D.C., or if a person possesses everything to make his or her earthly life happy. Without Christ, he or she is lost and has no future hope. A decision to reject Jesus will keep a person separated from Him for all of eternity. Nothing more than salvation in Christ has a more significant effect on life after death. How beautiful are the feet who bring good news, proclaiming peace [with God] and salvation in Christ. Yes, our God reigns and we share the news of His victory.

Jonah dragged his feet in being a blessing. Well, he did more than drag his feet. The man ran in the total opposite direction. He did not want to be the one to take the news to Nineveh.

What is the attitude of your heart when it comes to the lost?

As we develop our heart for journey and an open mind to the road that the Lord wants to take us down, allow Him to fill you with a radical love for others. The Father has children yet to come home, and the Lord wants to use *you* as His hands and feet. Will you allow Him? Will you open yourself to Him in this way? It sure makes the journey that much more exciting!

What do you think? Is Jonah ready to drop the "not my problem" attitude and follow God? Tomorrow, we'll dive deeper into this story and let me just tell you, things are going to get wet. Oh poor Jonah—he should have gone to Nineveh.

What is one way you will be a blessing to someone else today?

After you do it, come back and record how it went.

"Do not withhold good from those to whom it is due, when it is in the power of your hand to do so."

—PROVERBS 3:27 NKJV

Day Two

One early summer morning, I needed milkweed for our monarch caterpillars to eat. Peter was awake and in the basement, playing his video games. I walked downstairs, gave a verbal hi as I passed by, slid on Dan's Crocs, and opened the sliding door to go out and snip my milkweed.

Upon my return, I looked at Peter and was surprised to see him with a pair of nerdy prop glasses resting upon his face (the kind without any lenses). I stopped and chuckled—I didn't know why he was wearing them. But there he was, relaxed on the couch with pajama pants, a ball cap and the big fat glasses with masking tape in the center. He's such a funny kid! And then as quickly as I was entertained by the scene, I realized that I had greeted my child and gone outside without even looking at his precious face. I had been so focused on what I was doing that I walked by, said hi, and headed out the door without looking in his direction and making eye contact with this young man (who will be all grown up and out of our house before we know it!). Immediately, I was filled with remorse that I hadn't taken the time to see him, to truly notice and connect with him.

This experience was such a good reminder to my heart of how easy it can be to be preoccupied and so focused on our own things that we miss *seeing* others and their needs. As followers of Christ, we are called to serve others, to love radically, and to value people over tasks. And living a life of this magnitude will be so much more meaningful than just living for ourselves.

❖How is a heart to serve and a love for others initially demonstrated by the simple act of noticing people?

Are you good at noticing people or do you tend to be more preoccupied with other things?

Let's continue to look at our prodigal prophet who wasn't interested in taking the time to "see" the needs of an entire city, nor follow through on what God called him to do. Jonah wanted nothing to do with the Ninevites. He had no heart to serve. No open hands to help. No ready feet to take the message God gave him.

Open your Bibles and read Jonah 1:4–16. What did God send in verse 4 and what happened while Jonah was aboard?

Yesterday, we read that Jonah went down to Joppa to flee from God. We will notice the direction that Jonah went is mentioned several times in this section of the account—however, we are not talking north, south, east, or west. The direction is down. Jonah went *down* to Joppa. He went *down* in the boat and slept. In the next section, he will go *down* into the sea and eventually, *down* into the belly of the fish. What is the significance? May I suggest to you that when we are walking out of the will of God, there is nowhere to go but down.

Sure, we may be able to get a little sleep at first, but God won't allow His children too much comfort when we are in willful disobedience to His will and plan. And it isn't to punish the child, it is to bring His child back to Himself. Jonah was a prophet of the Most High God, the very Creator of the land and sea. God will use what He wants—whether an enormous storm or a great fish—to bring the heart of His child back to Himself and His purpose.

Now in our passage today, Jonah was conciliatory toward the sailors and instructed them to throw him overboard, but he still wasn't fully "on board" with God's agenda and plan. And that's a problem. Let's look at one who always did what the Father told Him (John 6:38, 14:31). His heart and His loving care for others will stand in stark contrast to the attitude and actions we've seen from Jonah.

> **Read Mark 5:21–43. Pay particular attention to Jesus' interaction with the different individuals involved in this account. Who were the two recipients of Jesus' touch and what were their previous conditions?**

I love the details that Mark provided for us in this passage. We see Jairus' desperation as he fell at the feet of Jesus, pleading for the life of his daughter, and making his request that the Lord put His hands on the girl. And Jesus accompanied him. The Lord saw this father's turmoil, and He cared.

Scripture then notes that a large crowd was closing in on Jesus. Can you picture it? Masses of people around Him. I remember trying to get through the hallway at my high school between classes. Boy, sometimes you could easily get lost in the crowd in those three minutes before the bell rang. But the woman with the issue of blood had such great faith that she pressed through the crowd and touched Jesus' cloak. After being discovered, she was filled with fear as she went before Him to confess her actions. Yet what did Jesus call her? Did He reprimand or rebuke her? Did He call her names? No, He called her daughter, acknowledged her faith, and sent her in peace.

Before Jesus could continue on to Jairus' house, they were informed that the little girl was dead. What did Jesus do then? Did He say, "Oh well, next job"? No, He told them not to be afraid and to believe. He encouraged them and gave them hope. (Did you notice which disciples He took inside the house with Him?) Once in the room, I love that Jesus took the hand of the girl—how sweet and tender. And not as if to leave the scene unfinished, Jesus then instructed the parents to give the child something to eat. How loving, compassionate, and thoughtful our God is!

We see over and over again throughout the Scriptures that Jesus saw people, and He cared for people. When the man with leprosy came into one of the towns to see Jesus, Jesus healed him (Luke 5:12–14). Remember lepers were secluded in their own communities; they were not supposed to be entering a town. So the fact that Jesus engaged with him was radical. When Jesus saw the widow of Nain processing in the funeral of her son, Scripture tells us that His heart went out to her, and He raised the young man (Luke 7:11–17). When the masses were hungry, Jesus fed them (John 6:1–15). When the Lord saw the despised chief tax collector Zacchaeus up in the sycamore tree, He showed kindness and love by going to his house as a guest. The effect it had on Zacchaeus was transforming. He gave half of his possessions to the poor and repaid anyone he cheated four-fold (Luke 19:1–10).

Whether it was the centurion looking for healing for his suffering servant (Matt. 8:5–13) or the company of Mary sitting at His feet listening (Luke 10:38–42), Jesus made time for people. The sick, the hurting, the paralyzed, the blind, the mute, the sinners, the unwanted, the unloved—even the rich and mighty—they all came to Jesus and He received them all.

People were not problems to Jesus. They were precious souls in need and worth His attention. They came from different backgrounds and had different stories. And each one was changed after an encounter with the Messiah. Yes, people were on His agenda.

Was Jonah interested in God's agenda? No, unfortunately not. And God is about to spin that disobedient prophet around—or should I say hurl him into the belly of the fish—until Jonah gets in line with the kingdom agenda God intended to release upon Nineveh.

Last spring, I was at Wal-Mart doing my grocery shopping. I noticed an older man fidgeting with his smart phone as he slowly came down the aisle. He was glancing around, obviously trying to find something and struggling. He had tried to call his wife for help and was talking to himself (something I do so much in stores these days!). I made a small comment about how hard it is to find things in the store when they keep switching things around, and then I asked what he was looking for. The man said sugar-free Jell-O. His wife used to do the shopping, but she was diagnosed with breast cancer, and so he took over the grocery shopping while she was ill.

"For the Son of Man came to seek and to save the lost."

—LUKE 19:10

I happened to be standing very close to the Jell-O, and so I pointed it out to him and then helped him look for the particular flavor his wife requested. He was tired and worn, and concern for his wife oozed out of each sentence. We chatted a moment, and I told him that I would pray for his wife. He expressed genuine appreciation and commented that he believed prayer worked. Just then, another woman coming down the aisle had overheard part of our conversation. She stopped and kindly asked the sweet man for his wife's name and told him that she was going to pray for her too! He was touched and so thankful.

To help and encourage this man didn't take any huge time out of my day. I didn't do anything all that significant. All I did was notice him and respond. But to him, the interaction between three strangers was powerful. The man was on the Lord's agenda that day—He knew that the man needed encouragement to persevere and to know he wasn't alone.

When we live by God's agenda, we value what God values. And He values people. He sees people right where they are and precisely what they need. Now, this doesn't mean it is always easy. Unlike my few minutes in the grocery store, self-sacrifice is often necessary. I am regularly trying to balance my "type A, task-oriented" self with a more people-oriented approach. I like my to-do list and I *really* like getting things done on my list. But what if by putting people first more often, I could introduce others to the goodness of my God simply with a little love, kindness, and intentional thoughtfulness? Whether or not I get something finished should never take priority when a heartbeat gets in the mix.

> A heart for journey lives by our Heavenly Father's agenda, fulfilling His will and purpose over our own.

As we wrap up today, allow me to ask you what I have been asking myself: whose agenda do you live by? Do you live like Jonah on your own or do you live according to one that fulfills the purpose and will of your Heavenly Father? In Luke 4:43, Jesus said, "I must proclaim the good news of the kingdom of God to the other towns also, because that is why I was sent." Jesus was sent to proclaim the good news. His feet were ready to do the will of His Father and the work of the kingdom.

You, my friend, are also called and being sent by the Father. Listen for His Spirit and don't drag your feet like Jonah. Oh yes, people are on the kingdom agenda today!

Week Four

✣ **How can you be more open to God's agenda and the ways that He wants to use you to help others?**

Has He laid anything on your heart to do?

> *"Fear the LORD and serve him faithfully with all your heart; consider what great things he has done for you."*
>
> —1 SAMUEL 12:24

Day Three

Well, we had quite the splash when Jonah hit the water and the seas grew calm yesterday. Did you notice how the sailors were in awe and feared Jonah's God? Even our disobedience and the way God rebukes us can be used as a witness for His power and glory. Not that I want to start a trend. After all, it is much more comfortable to bring God glory on the dry ground of obedience. Don't you think?

Jonah might not have been thrilled about the journey he was on or even about to go on. He had not set his heart on pilgrimage. He was avoiding the journey to Nineveh on which God was calling him. How about you? Is your heart becoming more established and open to the journey the Lord wants to take *you* on? I hope you are progressing not only in this, but also in memorizing Psalm 84:5. Let's check in on that.

Fill in the blanks below:

"_____ are those whose _____ is in _____, whose _____ are set on _____."

Psalm 84:5

Jonah's feet were being placed on a new section of road—only this one was going to be dark, damp, and quite the time to learn.

Read Jonah 1:17–2:10. Where was Jonah while he prayed?

We see in the last verse of chapter one, that God arranged this fish for Jonah. Different versions translate the verb as prepared, provided, or appointed. This was no accidental swallowing, no delicious-looking man randomly being hurled into the sea. This was the appointment of God for Jonah to meet the fish.

The book of Jonah with its account of the great fish is probably one of the most criticized books of the Bible because people have a hard time believing its veracity, sadly even among Christians.[67] But with stories of walls falling down at a shout, mighty seas being split, and the resurrection of the dead, I have no problem believing this story is true simply because I know the power and nature of our God. There truly is nothing He cannot do! And if He wanted a huge fish to swallow a man, it was certainly going to happen.

I would like to point out as well that Jesus Himself referred to and treated the account of Jonah as a fact. When asked by the Pharisees and teachers of the law for a sign, in Matthew 12:38–41, Jesus pointed to the sign of Jonah and said that just as Jonah was in the belly of the fish for three days and three nights, so will the Son of Man be in the heart of the earth. This was alluding to His coming death and resurrection.

Not to diminish the miraculous nature of Jonah and the fish, I would also like you to note a few things. For the Jew, any part of one day was treated as a whole day. The combination phrase "three days and three nights" need not refer to an actual 72-hour period.[68] I remember my Bible professor in college sharing stories of documented accounts of individuals being swallowed by various creatures of the sea and surviving, although none as long as Jonah.

In my research, I read of Dr. Harry Rimmer, President of the Research Science Bureau of Los Angeles, who documented a case of a man being swallowed by a huge rhinodon in the English Channel. He had been on a boat trying to harpoon the gigantic whale shark when he fell overboard and was swallowed. Forty-eight hours later, the shark was caught, and upon slitting open the creature, the man was found inside unconscious but alive. Dr. Rimmer met the man two years later in 1926 and noted that the survivor had yellow-brown patches all over his skin and "his body was devoid of hair."[69]

Even without accounts like this supporting the possibility of Jonah's story, we can believe and take God at His Word. And I am looking forward to hearing Jonah's version of the story in heaven! Maybe with three days in the stomach juices of the great fish bleaching his skin (as many scholars believe),[70] he will still be somewhat easy to recognize. Although, I suppose resurrection bodies will take care of that.

Back in chapter two, Jonah finally called on the Lord while in the belly of the fish. Even though he had run away, he knew God was gracious and forgiving. He saw the fish as God's means of saving him from a watery grave. Interestingly, Jonah said that he had been banished from God's sight despite the fact that he was the one running away. Yet he still spoke in hope that he would look upon God's temple again. Ah, the theme of the temple and God's presence appears profusely throughout the Old Testament.

In verse 6, we see a change of direction. No longer was Jonah heading down. Now God was bringing him up, bringing his life out of the pit. Jonah had learned the lesson. And in verse 9, Jonah offered praise, and the commitment to sacrifice and fulfill his vow.

At the end of Jonah 2:9, what does Jonah declare? Why do you think this is important?

Jonah learned his lesson (or at least he does for a time). The prophet will no longer run. At last, he will go to Nineveh. Let's do some of our own self-reflection

> *"For we are God's handiwork, created in Christ Jesus to do good works, which God prepared in advance for us to do."*
>
> —EPHESIANS 2:10

for a few moments. Ephesians 2:10 tells us that God has prepared good works for us to do. Just as the Lord called Jonah to a work, He has called you and me. And also like Jonah, it involves what is on His agenda—people.

So let's ask ourselves the hard questions. Are we living each day with a heart to serve? Do we have open hands to help and ready feet to go when He calls? Are we looking for opportunities to reach others with God's love? Do we notice people and take the time to invest in others, or do we tend toward selfish living? Are we sharing our faith in both indirect and direct ways? There is a mindset that is required to do this, and it comes down to how we view others.

✢How does the way we view others affect the way we serve?

What keeps you personally from the mindset of regularly serving others? Be as specific if you can.

A changing point for me was years ago when the Lord really started pressing on my heart that every person is created in the image of God and therefore, possesses great value. How can I not notice someone who has such value? Sadly, our world doesn't attribute this unique worth to people. Although when you think of who the prince of this world is, are you surprised?

Remember we have an enemy who wants to downplay not only the value of those around us and the difference we can make, but he also wants us to be focused on ourselves. If our outlook is centered on ourselves, we won't see others. But you'll know you have a victory in this when you can be in the midst of your own challenge or draining season of life, and you can still reach out and help someone else. In fact, I would venture to say that it is an incredible victory. Loving and serving other people, extending mercy and grace, and demonstrating the love of Jesus to others is a sign to our generation that Christians are more than angry, self-righteous individuals. As we show hospitality, generosity, and simple kindness, we will convince our world, albeit one person at a time, that the followers of Christ are worthy of His name.

Now, let's talk specifically about sharing our faith.

✵**Read 1 Peter 3:15. What are we supposed to be ready to share?**

Spiritual conversations can be intimidating to many people. We fear disapproval, conflict, or being thought of as foolish. We fear not having the right answers if pressed on difficult issues. I can so easily walk into a room and talk to a group of believers about the Lord and how He is moving, but my stomach can stir with butterflies when I'm trying to interject faith into a conversation with someone who I perceive wants nothing to do with the Lord. But let me remind myself and you—the results aren't up to us! They are fully and wholly up to God. Even with Jonah. He wasn't responsible for how Nineveh responded. He was just charged with taking the message.

✵**Is there a reason you are intimidated to share your faith with unbelievers? How can you overcome this?**

For the last few weeks in the adult Sunday School class at my church, various people have been sharing their personal testimonies. Because Dan and I think this is incredibly valuable for our high school students to hear, we have been attending the adult class as a group. It is so good for our young people to hear how God has worked and is working in peoples' lives—especially those they know. Not only does it build faith and point to Jesus, but it connects our hearts together and builds community (ah the beauty of community—you saw that coming, didn't you?).

Some of the individuals have written out their testimonies before sharing it (especially if this was the first time) so that they could stay focused and organized as they shared. And whether someone has given their testimony with or without notes, each one has been great!

Have you ever written out your testimony? Putting pen to paper is a beneficial practice and helps us to fulfill what 1 Peter 3:15 tells us to do—to be ready to share the reason for the hope we have. Not that you have to carry these notes around with you, but even the exercise of taking the time to write it out is very beneficial.

If you have never shared your testimony before or written it down, let's take the rest of our time today to get started. A testimony can involve several elements. It can include: what your life was like before Jesus became your Lord and Savior in comparison to after, the difference He has made in your life, what He saved you from, or what He did in your life. Some people have incredible and dramatic conversion stories, but it is okay if you don't. I was a child when I was saved—I don't remember the day of my salvation. All salvation experiences include recognizing your need for Him, repenting of sin, and walking in new life in Christ. But everyone has different paths, journeys, and experiences with the Lord. My testimony includes the basics of salvation, but it is more focused on what He did in my life after being saved, even years down the road. I can share of the great hope, purpose, and direction He has lavishly given—how He has moved in challenging situations of my life and been with me the whole time. The key is that your testimony is personal to you.

Start writing your testimony here.

Let me encourage you to continue working on this and make a point to share it with someone in the next few weeks. If you are doing this study with a group, consider sharing a couple of testimonies when you meet or adding on an extra night at the end of the study to hear everyone's testimonies.

Sharing our faith with others, especially in the climate of our culture, can be very hard. But I want to leave you with something my pastor recently said for those times when you think someone isn't interested in hearing about God, and you are intimidated to share. He said not to go into the conversation thinking that *they're not looking for Jesus*. Rather, what we need to remember is that *He* may be looking for *them*.

> A heart for journey shares our faith in both direct and indirect ways, because others need to hear of God's love.

Day Four

Today is the day of second chances. I'm so thankful our God does not dismiss us after one mistake. The Bible is full of second chances (and thirds and fourths . . .) with people like Abraham, David, Peter, Paul, and yes, our good pal Jonah. Today, Jonah finally gets in step with God's plan. We will see Jonah journey over five hundred miles to the spiritually-lost city of Nineveh. How will they respond? What then will Jonah do afterwards? Well, we'll have to wait until tomorrow for some of that. But let's just say Jonah wasn't the happiest kid on the block when it came to the graciousness of God's mercy.

> ✶ Read Jonah 3:1–10. We see that the word of the Lord came to Jonah a _____ time. What did Jonah do this time according to verse 3?

Jonah's journey to Nineveh likely took about a month by caravan.[71] That is quite a long time to consider his calling, his disobedience, and the God who saved him from drowning and prepared a fish just for him (and obviously we're not talking about dinner). Hopefully, the stink of the fish had now worn off, but many believe Jonah's skin still would have likely been bleached by the gastric juices.[72] Add that to the possibility of all his hair being gone . . . well, you get the picture.

This reminds me of the time my friend shared her experience of mixing the chemicals for their hot tub. The first time her husband soaked in the water following the chemical treatment, his orange swim trunks turned purple, and he lost all of his leg hair. Oh, the image of him stepping out!

I'm guessing Jonah was quite the sight as he graced the gates of the city of Nineveh. But at least, Jonah was finally following God's instructions. He may not have felt any love for the people of Nineveh, but he sure felt the need for obedience to the Lord Almighty and his prophetic calling. And so, he went and preached. He told the Ninevites that in forty days, the city would be destroyed. With the lack of character and integrity of the Assyrians, I am curious why the brutal Ninevites didn't try to kill Jonah on the spot. Maybe they had heard of the prophet and his adventure at sea and the God whom he served. The Hebrews were known for being monotheistic so the God who chastened Jonah was the same God of the message he was preaching. Or maybe the Ninevites' acceptance of the prophet had to do with Jonah's appearance sparking a respect and fear of his God in their hearts. Proverbs does tell us that "the fear of the LORD is the beginning of wisdom" (Prov. 9:10).

> *"God's purpose of grace cannot be frustrated."*
>
> —J. Vernon McGee[73]

What was the people's response in verses 5–9?

They humbled themselves and fasted. The king instructed everyone to call on God and to lay aside their evil ways and violence. And they did. Some scholars differ on whether they think this is true conversion or not. They question whether the Ninevites laid aside their pagan gods. And I can't say for sure, but I do know that whatever their hearts and their true response, God saw it and relented in sending calamity.

This brings into play another possible reason Jonah may have been reluctant to bring God's message of judgement to Nineveh. As we talked about earlier, Jonah knew that if God was willing to offer the warning, He was likely willing to relent from destroying the city upon their repentance. Jonah may have felt that this put his status as a prophet in Israel at risk. Afterall, when a prophet spoke, words were fulfilled. This was one of the ways the people knew if a man was a true prophet (Deut. 18:21–22).[74] What would the people of Israel think when Jonah's prophesy against Nineveh failed? Jonah, however, was not only missing the fact that this was a conditional prophetic word, but he was also caring about the opinion of the wrong person(s). I would like to suggest that Jonah cared more about his reputation and the acceptance of others than he did about the approval of the Most High.

Do you worry about what others think more often than you should?

A friend and I were at a flea market shopping at a booth with a woman who was selling stones, gems, and arrowheads. My daughter has always had an interest in geology, so I was buying an arrowhead for her collection. The woman came over to the table to talk with us and other customers, and she mentioned that "nature" gives us what we need with precious stones (definitely leaning toward the new age idea of healing stones and crystals). My friend without hesitation kindly answered, "The Lord does give us exactly what we need." She wasn't contributing to the new age idea, but rather bringing the conversation to a focus on God. The woman quickly and whole-heartedly agreed and then talked about the fact that she was just diagnosed with breast cancer and would be having a biopsy the following week. We told her we would pray for her.

We began walking down the road, flanked with people and booths on both sides, and I looked at my friend and said, "We should have prayed with her. Let's go back." So we made a u-turn and stepped behind the table to be close to the woman, and I asked her if we could pray for her. You never know how a person is going to respond to something like this, but she willingly agreed. And my friend and I prayed for this woman in the name of Jesus. When we were done, she commented on her goosebumps and expressed her appreciation.

Early the next morning, I laid in one of the beds in our hotel room (this was a huge flea market that warranted an overnight girls' getaway) thinking we should go back and give her a Bible. I don't usually travel with my regular study Bible—it's so big and heavy. Normally, I just travel with a smaller one, so we decided to take that one to her.

I wrote a note in the front of the Bible and that morning, we searched for the booth. With over 2,000 vendors, we figured it might be tricky, but we prayed, and the Lord answered our prayer. There she was standing behind the table with her rocks and gems. I asked her if she had a Bible and offered her the one in my hands. She took it—somewhat indifferently. And I don't know if she ever opened a page. But I pray she did or that she will, when the Lord prepares her heart. I pray for her salvation and her faith, and that the Lord heals her and uses this season to draw her to Himself.

Responses are always tricky when we are sharing about God. It is easy to fear the response. It takes boldness to say what needs to be shared. And there are times when we will never find out what happened in a person's life afterward. I think of all the missionaries around the globe who will be joyously surprised when greeted in heaven by those affected by their message both directly and indirectly, despite the fact that they felt like there was no fruit during their time on earth. I have faithful friends who have spent many years on the mission field and while seeds were planted in those early years in ministry, they are only now, in these last few years, seeing great fruit. To God be the glory!

✣**Have you had opportunities to share your faith? How did it go?**

Don't ever worry if an opportunity feels too small, if you only were able to share a little, or even about the results. Those are up to the Lord. We are just called to lovingly bring the good news and sometimes, it just means planting seeds. As we share our lives with people, building community, and radically loving others with a heart to serve, I believe the Lord will open doors. Opportunities will arise. So, be the church. Tell someone that you are praying for them. Give them a reason for your hope. Don't worry if they are resistant, quiet, or antagonistic. Pray for boldness, love them, and place them in the hands of God.

When we live beyond ourselves with a heart to serve, when we live to be the hands and feet of Jesus, when we radically love others, our journeys become so much more exciting. It's always an adventure with God. Who knows where you'll meet someone who needs to hear about Jesus? Maybe you'll be the one to introduce him or her to the Savior.

> **Write a prayer asking God for boldness, opportunities, and a passion for the lost.**

Ah, I think your feet are looking more beautiful! . . . I'll go call Aunt Tara and tell her.

Day Five

Well here we are at the end of week 4. There is so much we have learned already and I am praying that God is giving us a heart to serve and a heart for the lost as we journey with Him. As I am writing this lesson, the Jewish high holy day, Yom Kippur, begins tomorrow night. Yom Kippur is the Day of Atonement and considered to be the most holy day on the Jewish calendar. This was the one day each year on which the High Priest would enter the Holy of Holies in the temple to make atonement for the people. Since the Jews have not had a temple since its destruction in 70 AD, the sacrifices have not been made. But rabbis in the first century instituted substitutions of prayer, repentance, and charity for the sacrifices that were supposed to be offered as the holy day was observed.[75]

Many Scriptures are read during Yom Kippur, but there is only one book that is read in its entirety. Can you guess which book will be read in synagogues by Jews around the world? The book of Jonah. Yes, the whole story will be recounted to his people.

There are three holy days in the first month of Tishri on the Hebrew calendar with the second being Yom Kippur. The first is Rosh Hashanah (the Feast of Trumpets or Yom Teruah), ten days earlier, which begins a period of repentance and reflection. The time of introspection then concludes with Yom Kippur—the day of Atonement. Rabbis today point to Jonah being read on Yom Kippur because it reminds us that no one can escape God's judgement, and that God's mercy is still shown when repentance takes place,[76] as was the case with Nineveh. God's mercy to Nineveh is a lesson for us as sinners still today.

You can see then how Jonah fits right in with Yom Kippur and its themes of judgement, repentance, "atonement and regeneration."[77]

Let's dive into the final chapter of Jonah. Please read Jonah 4:1–4. What was Jonah's state of mind at this point in the account?

❖**What does Jonah say he knew about God?**

This man was not happy! In fact, he was so angry that he says he would rather die than live and see Nineveh saved. And he will wish for his death three times in the chapter. Have you ever been so angry? To me, this passage is characterized by a combination of a child's fit and an attempt at manipulation.

Read verses 5–11. What did Jonah build in verse 5?

Now, stay with me because I want you to see something pretty cool. The Hebrew word for what Jonah built is *sukkah*, which means booth. The third major holy day taking place this month following Rosh Hashanah and Yom Kippur is Sukkot, the Feast of Tabernacles (Booths).

Turn to Leviticus 23:42–43. What did God instruct His people to do and what was the purpose?

After the first year in the wilderness following the exodus, the Hebrews celebrated the Feast of Tabernacles. The festival was tied to the celebration of the harvest, but we see in Leviticus 23, that the purpose was to tell their descendants that the Lord was the one who brought the Israelites out of Egypt. It commemorated the Hebrews' journey from Egypt to Sinai. And every year, the Israelites built booths for this festival.

Jonah should have spent time each year building a booth to commemorate God delivering His people out of the slavery and bondage they experienced in Egypt.[78] It was a reminder of being saved by the Lord's gracious hand. And yet, sitting under that symbol of God's saving power and care, what was Jonah's attitude? Jonah's people had been saved, but Jonah didn't want God extending the same grace, mercy, and saving power to Nineveh that his own people had received.

We have been saved by grace through the blood of Jesus, the Messiah. We have been the benefactors of God's incredible mercy, and we did nothing to earn it! We have received blessing after blessing. Do we ever withhold that from others? Do we long for God to deliver judgement while we have experienced such mercy?

How easy is it for you to extend kindness, mercy, and forgiveness to others, especially to those who have wounded or betrayed you?

Does (or should) your answer change when you consider what you have been given in Christ Jesus?

When I read verse five about Jonah finding a spot east of the city and waiting to see what was going to happen to Nineveh, I have to wonder if he wasn't looking for a show. Was he hoping for fire and brimstone? Was he hoping the earth would swallow up the depraved city like Korah and his friends? Was he hoping for complete and utter destruction? Yes, I think he was. I think Jonah's heart was very hard toward the Ninevites. Sure, he had finally obeyed God physically by walking through Nineveh with the Lord's message, but he hadn't gotten any closer to the message in his heart. He was extremely upset and downright angry. And look what happened when God provided a vine to shade Jonah and then the next day, a worm ate it. The ping pong ball of Jonah's emotions wavered between "very happy" and being so angry that he wanted to die.

What do you think God's reprimand at the end of the book of Jonah was all about?

Not only do we see Jonah's hardened heart laid bare, but we also see that he was finding fault with who God was: "a gracious and compassionate God, slow to anger and abounding in love, a God who relents from sending calamity" (Jon. 4:2). [79] How is that for self-assertion? Jonah's display in this last chapter also points greatly to his selfishness. It was all about *him*. His vine. His life. His thoughts on what should have happened. His anger and what he knew about God. If we are only thinking of ourselves, we will not be open to what God wants to do in us and through us. Selfishness not only sits diabolically opposite of a heart to serve, but it also diminishes our ability to be wildly used by God. It's right where the enemy of our souls wants us. But as followers of Christ, we make room for others in our lives. We look for opportunities to be the light in a dark place. Instead of waiting and watching for fire to fall from heaven, we could be the spark that God uses to draw people to Himself.

If God had called you to Nineveh, would it have been a struggle for you? Take a moment and ponder this.

> Instead of waiting and watching for fire to fall from heaven, we could be the spark that God uses to draw people to Himself.

Living for others is no easy task. It can complicate our lives and may even mean dying to self and our own desires. There will be times when we have to step out of the comfort and security to which we are accustomed, make sacrifices, and live above fear. But it is all for a purpose—extending the love of the Father to a world in need. Sharing the good news of the Gospel by maintaining open hands and ready feet, and developing what author Rosaria Butterfield calls "contagious grace."

> The key to contagious grace—the grace that allows [those in] the margins to move to the center, that commands you to never fear the future,

the grace that reveals that what humbles you cannot hurt you if Jesus is your Lord—that grace is ours when we do what Mary says to do . . . In John 2:5, she says to the servants (and the Holy Spirit says to us), 'Do whatever He tells you.'[80]

What does Jesus tell us? Turn to Mark 8:34–37 and record the answer.

Oh yes, my friend, we could gain the whole world, but what good is that for all of eternity? None. Absolutely none! Build up treasures in heaven (Matt. 6:19–20). Have compassion. Love others. Win the lost. God can use anyone, and He wants to use you! Do you have a heart to serve? Do you have open hands and ready feet? He is looking and He will provide in you what is needed for every encounter.

"For the eyes of the LORD range throughout the earth to strengthen those whose hearts are fully committed to him." 2 Chronicles 16:9

A heart for journey is open to what God wants to do in us and through us.

✢**As we look back at the book of Jonah, what has been your greatest takeaway from this week?**

Ah, so much more we could say about Jonah and so many angles we could take, but our time is almost up on this leg of our journey. I hope you are enjoying it as much as I am!

See you in the video!

WATCH THE WEEK 4 VIDEO

More Than Garments

Scriptures in this Session: Acts 9:36–42, Isaiah 58:6–12

Also mentioned: Isaiah 26:8

Tabitha is first identified as a _____ of Christ.

Tabitha's _____ for Jesus and her commitment to Him spilled out into a _____ for others.

How do we love like this?

- Be _____.
- Love with sincerity and _____.
- Avoid a _____ and prideful heart.
- Follow the greatest _____.

Jesus is our ultimate example for _____ others.

Three Questions to Ask Yourself:

- Does my love for Jesus overflow into a love for people?
- Do I seek to love and welcome others even when it means pushing beyond my normal routine or comfort zone?
- Does my love for others point back to Jesus and bring glory to God?

Video lessons are available at KristenTiber.com/AHeartForJourneyVideos.

Week Five

The Road Ahead

*"So is my word that goes out from my mouth:
It will not return to me empty, but will accomplish what
I desire and achieve the purpose for which I sent it.
You will go out in joy and be led forth in peace;
the mountains and hills will burst into song before you,
and all the trees of the field will clap their hands.
Instead of the thornbush will grow the juniper
and instead of briers the myrtle will grow.
This will be for the LORD's renown,
for an everlasting sign, that will endure forever."*

Isaiah 55:11–13

Day One

As I am writing this week's lesson, my family is vacationing in Gatlinburg, Tennessee. This is our first time visiting the area and so far, it has been a very nice trip, but we made one major mistake. We booked a condo up in the mountains—as in winding, mountain roads to get to the condo. As in no guard rails nor shoulders on the winding, mountain roads. As in cliff-side drops if you cross over the white line . . . well, that is *if* there is a white line. There are switchback curves with multiple roads coming into those intersections, inclines so steep they would make great ski hills, and roads so narrow you hope only a small car will come in the opposite direction. I knew there would be mountain roads, but I never expected anything like this.

The first time we drove up the mountain, I was driving because I get carsick on curvy roads, especially when someone else is doing the driving. I don't like driving up and down big hills to begin with, but these were terrifying! It didn't help that when we arrived at the top, there was a burning smell coming from the car. And as quickly as I felt immensely thankful that we had safely arrived, it was just a matter of seconds before I realized that we would have to do it over and over again as we came and went throughout the entire week.

The thought sent fear through my entire body. How would I drive that again? I felt stuck. I felt trapped. Tears streamed down my face. On one hand I didn't want to leave the condo at all until the blessed day we would go down the mountain for good. But on the other hand, if I stayed in the condo, I would miss all the fun things we had planned for the week. This may sound extreme, but this is exactly how I felt.

As I sat at the table looking out over the view (that we had prized over local access to everything else—*on flat ground*), I hadn't felt so fearful in a very long time. Fear of when you have no control over a situation. Fear of no options. Fear that consumes every cell in your body. Knowing I had to go up and down that mountain who knows how many times that week . . . it didn't seem doable.

And I knew God had allowed this because just that day, we were listening to messages that talked about stepping out of your comfort zone like Abraham when he was called to leave his family and hometown, and travel to a land that God was giving him. I knew I was going to have to push through.

I looked out the window that night at the Smoky Mountains, and boy, they were beautiful. They're vast, big, and far reaching. I thought of Moses walking up the desert mountain to meet with God and then returning, finding the people worshiping the golden calf. What fear Moses must have felt in the responsibility of millions of people for whom he was in charge of leading. And yet, up on the mountain was his strength and the incredible time he had spent with the Lord.

A sign hung on the condo wall between the windows overlooking the mountains. It read, "Be strong and courageous." I knew where that came from—when Joshua had to cross the Jordan river.

> **In fact, let's turn there now. Read Joshua 1:1–9. Why was Joshua the new leader of the Israelites, and what did God instruct him to do?**

> ✣**What kinds of things tend to make you fearful?**

> ✣**Why do you think God instructed Joshua three times in that passage to be strong and courageous?**

Fear can be a very tricky thing. Even the next day, when Dan drove down the hill (and by then we remembered we should have been in a lower gear), I was a nervous wreck going down the mountain—bracing myself in the car, trying to take slow, long breaths. Thankfully, Dan was going nice and slow, and not just for me but for safety reasons. We also took a different road at one point, which allowed for us to avoid the three most nasty turns with seventy-degree inclines.

But that whole day, there was one underlying thought with me—we have to go back up. *We have to go back up.* It was as if someone had taken a piece of fear-filled sticky fly paper and put the strip from my head to my toe. I wasn't shaking it off. The fear came with me to Anakeesta, a beautiful park with ski lift rides to a mountain top village filled with shopping, amazing tree top canopy bridges, and a lookout tower. The fear accompanied me as we shopped in downtown Gatlinburg. The fear was my guest at lunch. And even when we drove out toward Pigeon Forge and rode an alpine mountain coaster, it was there looming in my mind. As much as I wanted to fling that fear off, it was not going away. My eyes would well up with tears at just the thought of having to drive up the mountain. And I prayed. Even in the middle of the night, I laid in bed praying for the fear to go in Jesus' name. But I couldn't shake it off. I knew I was going to have to step out of my comfort zone. I knew I was going to have to "be strong and courageous."

When have you felt *consumed* by fear?

The last time I remember this kind of fear taking over my body was my first c-section when I had to hug a nurse while the anesthesiologist gave me the spinal. The fear of not knowing what to expect and being cut wide open *while I was awake* was enough to make me shake from head to toe. At least I got a baby at the end of the ordeal. There was no such prize for making it up and down the mountain.

Joshua was filling a large void after Moses died. He was now in charge of a massive amount of people. He had to lead them across the Jordan River, a river that had a very strong current, capable of taking even a strong swimmer several yards down river during a crossing,[81] not to mention it was at flood stage during the harvest (Josh. 3:15). He was about to enter a land that God was giving them, and yet, it was filled with people who would oppose them. They would do battle. But Joshua would battle not only with the inhabitants of the land, but also with the Israelites who didn't have the best track record of faithfulness. Joshua would need to be strong and courageous!

As we look back in Joshua 1, notice with me the beautiful literary nature of what the Lord told Joshua in verses 5b-9. Now, I am not someone who especially loves poetry per se, but I can appreciate the emphasis that God placed in this passage. Below is what my Biblical Theology Study Bible shares in the notes on this passage. Can you find the parallels? Fill in the blanks using Joshua 1:5b-9.

    a I will never _____ you nor forsake you.

        b Be strong and _____ . . .

            c Be _____ and very courageous.

                d Be careful to _____ all the law . . .

                    e Keep the Book of the law . . .

                    e' meditate on it day and night . . .

                d' be careful to _____ everything written in it.

            c' Be _____ and courageous.

        b' Do not be _____; do not be discouraged . . .

    a' _____ will be with you wherever you go.[82]

> *"Fear and faith cannot live in the same heart, for fear always blinds the eyes to the presence of the Lord."*
>
> —Warren W. Wiersbe[83]

Let's look at this a little more in depth. Notice with me that the structure is repetitive, starting and ending with the presence of God. Remember back to Ezra and Nehemiah? The gracious hand of God was with them. God's presence is with us as well!

Read Matthew 28:18–20. What did Jesus promise His followers?

Even when I was on the mountain roads or just thinking about having to drive those roads, I had to remind myself that Jesus was with me. God is with us—wherever we go! Think about that for a moment. He is with you when you go about your normal daily routine. He is with you when you step out of your comfort zone. He is with you when you deal with the little annoyances of life, and He is with you when you face the serious, most difficult challenges life can offer. He is with you—always. Until the end of the age.

What comfort does it bring you to know that God is always with you on this journey of life?

> God will never instruct us to do something that He will not also help and empower us to do.

We also see that God instructed Joshua multiple times to be strong and courageous and not to be afraid nor discouraged. God will never instruct us to do something that He will not also help and empower us to do. Just as Jonah knew that if God was sending him to prophesy to Nineveh, He also stood ready to save Nineveh if the people repented. We can know that God will not call us to do something that He is not prepared to help us accomplish. If He has told us to be strong, and we apply our heart to this, He will help us to be strong.

> *"The will of God will never lead you where the grace of God can't keep you and the power of God can't use you."*
>
> —Warren W. Wiersbe[84]

On those mountain roads, you better believe I was thinking about 2 Timothy 1:7 in which Paul told Timothy that we have not been given a spirit of fear, but rather power, love, and a sound mind. And that falls right into the heart of the structure in Joshua 1:5b-9. The pinnacle of this poetic movement is on the

Word of God—keeping the law and meditating on it. When we are facing fear, we always have the Word of God. But we need to know the Word of God to be able to pull from it.

✣ **Do you have key verses you rely on when faced with fear?**

Turn to 1 Corinthians 10:13. How does this passage bring hope and encouragement?

This was the other verse on my mind when I was tempted to let fear reign. I asked God to provide me with a way out or a way to stand up under the fear. I was hoping the "way out" was that the rental company could switch us to another one of their properties that wasn't atop the winding, mountain roads. But that didn't work out.

Do you know what my way out was—the way I could stand up under the fear? It was sitting in the back seat, ear buds blasting praise music, remedies taken for motion sickness, and simply not looking. Ok occasionally, I peeked up and became nervous all over again. But last night as Dan drove up those mountain roads, I made it. I made it up without feeling afraid. I made it without tearing up. I made it because God gave me a way to stand up under the fear. Yes, we are going to drive those roads another seven or eight times as we come and go, but by the grace of God, I won't be afraid. I will be strong and courageous.

Please turn back briefly to Joshua, chapter 3. I want you to see something else that is pretty cool. The chapter starts out with the officers going through the camp to give instructions about crossing the Jordan River.

> **What did Joshua tell the people in verse 5? "Consecrate yourselves, for tomorrow the LORD will do _____ _____ among you."**

And He did amazing things among the people! When the priests carrying the ark of the covenant stood in the water of the Jordan River, the water stopped flowing from upstream. The people (who had heard of their ancestors crossing the Red Sea on dry ground) were now experiencing the miraculous hand of God in their life, in their moment of need, and on their own journey.

In verse 7, the Lord spoke again to Joshua. He said, "Today I will begin to exalt you in the eyes of all Israel, so they may **know that I am with you** as I was with Moses," [emphasis mine].

There it is again—God's presence. The people would *know* that the Lord was with Joshua. My friend, the Lord is with you. Sometimes, it can be hard to bring that thought fully home. But what if you could? What if you could live each day and each moment with that thought? He will *never* leave nor forsake you. He has promised that. Whether you are facing the mountain roads in Tennessee or the mountain roads of life, He has spoken and He is faithful to His Word. Fear is not your inheritance, child of God. No, we have "the incomparable riches of his grace, expressed in his kindness to us in Christ Jesus" (Eph. 2:7).

> **How can internalizing the thought that God is always with you give you confidence and courage on your journey?**

A heart for journey battles fear and presses for victory in Christ.

Day Two

How has the way you view life as a journey changed these last few weeks? As we have traveled with various sojourners in the Scriptures, have you been able to apply different principles to your own life? Oh, how I would love to chat with you and hear where you've been on your journey and how our God has sustained and provided for you.

Today, we are going to start our time in the Word with Psalm 121. This psalm is one of fifteen psalms that are known to be travel songs. Psalms 120–134 are called the "songs of ascent"[85] or "songs of degrees."[86] This series of psalms was sung by travelers on their way to Jerusalem. Scholars believe the Jewish people likely sang these songs as they returned to Israel after the exile, on the way to Jerusalem to celebrate the three annual feasts,[87] and possibly even as they went up the steps of the temple—one psalm for each step.[88] And they are called "songs of ascent" because geographically, you always went *up* to Jerusalem. These psalms are songs for journey!

> **While our focus will be on the first few verses, please read Psalm 121:1–8. Jot down what may have been helpful for a traveler to be reminded of while singing this song.**

As we start this psalm, we notice that the psalmist is looking to the mountains. To which mountains is he looking? The mountains of Jerusalem. And he proceeds to ask and answer his own question, *"Where does my help come from?"* As the psalmist's eyes are drawn up, it's not the mountains themselves that bring him help, but rather the One who dwells on the mountain of Jerusalem. The One who dwells in the temple. The One who has set His name in Jerusalem and established it as His dwelling place.

When we were driving in Tennessee, the mountain that we had to drive up and down brought nothing but fear. For me, the mountains were the source of fear. But the psalmist is looking to the mountain of God's special presence. God was the source of his help.

How did the psalmist describe God here in verse 2?

One of the best things we can do on this journey is to keep the proper perspective of who God is. He is the Maker of heaven and earth. He is a big, mighty, and powerful God, and as we know, there is nothing He can't do!

Our God created the stars and the planets, and set them into motion. He tells the ocean waves where to stop (Job 38:10–11). He is the Ancient of Days, the Alpha and Omega, and the bright Morning Star (Dan. 7:9, Rev. 22:13, 16). He is Savior, Redeemer, the Bread of Life and the Good Shepherd (Luke 2:11, Job 19:25, John 6:35, John 10:14). And what's more, He loves you! He calls you His own.

✣Does it help on our journeys to think about who God is? If so, how?

If you are looking for a new passage to memorize, Psalm 121 is a beautiful, encouraging, and hope-filled psalm to try next. The psalmist knew the road to Jerusalem could be a dangerous one, whether by conditions and terrain or with thieves and robbers.[89] Yet the whole psalm speaks to God's ability and interest in protecting and keeping the traveler while on his journey.

Have you ever walked a ragged path? One where you had to be careful where you stepped? I imagine there were parts of the road to Jerusalem that may not have been the easiest to navigate. Yet the psalmist is confident in God's ability to keep his foot from slipping.

Turn to Psalm 40:1–3. From where did the Lord lift David, and where did He set David's feet?

We have now been in our current house for seven years. It's a wonderful home, and we have been very blessed. But that first year here, the yard . . . it was a mud pit. From front to back and side to side, it was one giant mud pit of a yard. And if you've built a new house, you probably know what I'm talking about.

When the kids would play *outside*, they would track mud *inside*. I was at the point where I didn't even want to go out myself because the mud was so bad! And that first spring with all the rain made the terrain even worse. You know how it is when you take a step and the mud just sucks your foot in? Then when you pull it out, your foot is caked with mud on all sides? That was our yard. It was a mess! During that spring, we built a tree house in the woods. The problem was that you had to trek across the muddy back yard in order to get to the woods and the kids wanted to be out there all the time. So Dan placed large stepping stones in the mud to help them get across. And it made all the difference!

In Psalm 40, David talked about the mud and the mire, and about being in a slimy pit. Life can be muddy sometimes, can't it? David faced a lot in his lifetime between a king trying to kill him, his own son vying for the throne, and more. I don't think anyone gets through life without, at some point, feeling the mud cake up on his or her feet, making each step heavier and more challenging.

Can you think of a time you felt like you were in the mud and mire? How did you handle the situation?

But here is the hope. David cried out to the Lord for help. When we feel like we are standing in the mud, before anything else, we can turn to God, cry out, and wait for Him. He will hear our cry. God takes our feet and puts them on the rock. He gives us a firm place to stand.

Psalm 34:17 says "The righteous cry out, and the Lord hears them; he delivers them from all their troubles." David certainly knew something about troubles. But he also knew that God would deliver him. And so it is in his faithful God that David put his trust.

Read 2 Samuel 22:2–3 in the margin. In David's song of praise, who does David identify as his rock?

> "The LORD is my rock, my fortress and my deliverer; my God is my rock, in whom I take refuge, my shield and the horn of my salvation. He is my stronghold, my refuge and my savior . . ."
>
> —2 SAMUEL 22:2–3A

Not only does God keep our feet from slipping and give us a firm place to stand, but we see that He Himself is also the rock on which we stand! Read the verses in 2 Samuel again. There is no doubt that David finds sure footing, security, and safety in the Lord, his rock.

✢**Can you think of a time when the Lord has been your rock?**

Read 2 Samuel 22:31–37 (NIV 1984) below and fill your name in the blanks.

As for God, his way is perfect; the word of the LORD is flawless. He is a shield for all who take refuge in him. For who is God besides the LORD? And who is the Rock except our God? It is God who arms

_____ with strength and makes _____'s way perfect. He makes _____'s feet like the feet of a deer; he enables _____ to stand on the heights. He trains _____'s hands for battle; _____'s arms can bend a bow of bronze. You give _____ your shield of victory; you stoop down to make _____ great. You broaden _____'s path beneath [her], so that _____'s ankles do not turn.

Isn't that beautiful? I am filled with hope for the muddy seasons of life when I read that God is not just a shield and rock, but *my* shield and rock. He arms *me* with strength. He enables *me* to stand. He trains *my* hands. And notice what He does to the path beneath our feet? He broadens it. We aren't left trying to balance on some skinny, little, wobbly stone. No, the path on which we stand is wide and able to sustain.

There have been many times in my life when I was in the midst of the mud and mire, and Jesus put my feet on the rock and gave me a firm place to stand. He lifted the burden and scraped the mud from my feet. And He will do this for you too. When life is muddy around you—from the trivial things all hitting at once to the serious, life-changing events, the Lord will give you a firm place to stand. We can know and trust this.

In Ephesians 2:19–22, we are told by Paul that Jesus is the chief cornerstone. In 1 Peter 2:6, Peter quotes Isaiah 28:16 in reference to Jesus as the "chosen and precious cornerstone, and the one who trusts in him will never be put to shame." Whatever we face, wherever we walk, we can trust Him. He is strong and secure, and He doesn't change.

So what is the verdict? Is the woman who is set on the Rock secure? Is she able to stand?

If you feel like you are on the rocky terrain or in the midst of the mud today, how does this thought encourage you?

Look back at Psalm 40:5 because I think this is a beautiful conclusion to our study today. Wouldn't it be wonderful if we could join David as we live out our journeys and say, "Many, O LORD my God, are the wonders you have done. The things you planned for us no one can recount to you; were I to speak and tell of them, they would be too many to declare" Psalm 40:5 (NIV 1984).

> A heart for journey makes the Lord it's Rock in all circumstances.

I picture those rocks that Dan laid out across our yard—they enabled us to safely cross. They didn't take the mud away. But they gave us a firm place to stand. Our stability is in the cornerstone, Jesus. We can safely cross the terrain when we are found in Him. He will keep us from slipping. He will put our feet upon the Rock and give us a firm place to stand. And oh the wonders that are yet to be declared! Let's praise Him for His goodness!

Day Three

As we are drawing near to the end of our study, I would like to spend some time on a man who was quite the traveler in the years after Jesus' death and resurrection. Initially, he was vehemently opposed to the church and the cause of Christ. He himself oversaw the death of martyrs including Stephen in Acts 7:54–8:1. But you see, God can change anyone and He can use anyone no matter who they are or what they have done. And we will see how this individual once having encountered the risen Lord keeps on going despite setback after setback.

Turn to Acts 9:1–9. What was Saul's intent toward the believers in Damascus?

What was the movement of Christianity called in verse 2?

Damascus was a hub of a larger commercial network reaching into north Syria, Mesopotamia, Anatolia, Persia, and Arabia. If Christianity blossomed here, it would have quick and far-reaching effects.[90] So Saul set out for Damascus to imprison those who belonged to the Way.

I find it beautifully ironic that the movement of believers is called the Way here in Acts. The word in the Greek is *hodos*, and according to Strong's Concordance, its usage is as "a way, road, journey, path."[91] The Way likely referred to "the way to be saved" or "the way of the Lord" (based on Acts 16:17 and Acts 18:25–26).[92] Christianity most definitely is the way to be saved, but we can also see how the path or journey continues beyond the moment of salvation. This Way is a life path of seeking the road the Lord has for you, yielding to His will, and following Him until your earthly journey comes to an end. And for Saul, his path was about to intersect with the Messiah Himself.

What happened to Saul on the road to Damascus?

When Saul met Jesus, his path changed. The man who had so aggressively persecuted those of the Way became a fellow sojourner and spent the rest of his life for the cause of Christ. Let's look at what Saul did following his roadside detour.

Read Acts 9:10–19. What did the Lord tell Ananias in verse 15?

Would you have been apprehensive to meet Saul knowing his reputation? What do you think about the way the Lord worked in this situation?

Following his conversion, Saul spent several days with the disciples in Damascus and began preaching at once that Jesus was the Son of God (Acts 9:19–20). People were astonished, although some Jews conspired to kill him. He was rescued by his new friends who lowered him in a basket through an opening in the wall (Acts 9:23–25). I don't know—this is a scene I would have loved to see! New convert, adult male being lowered in a basket!

Upon his arrival in Jerusalem and once he gained the trust of the disciples, he preached fearlessly in the name of Jesus. But again, an attempt on Saul's life was made so the believers sent him to his hometown of Tarsus (Acts 9:29–30). Eventually, Barnabas brought Saul to Antioch, and the two taught and met with the church for a year (Acts 11:25–26).

Read Acts 12:25–13:3. What did the Holy Spirit speak to the church at Antioch, and what did the leaders do in response?

"Although I am less than the least of all the Lord's people, this grace was given me: to preach to the Gentiles the boundless riches of Christ . . ."

—EPHESIANS 3:8

From here on out, we will call this man Paul as he started using his Greek name Paul (from the Latin Paulus) instead of Saul, his Hebrew name. The subtle change happened in Acts 13:13 as he was setting sail on a missionary journey.[93] This isn't a name change, but rather a shift from one of his names to another (Acts 13:9).

In the passage just read, the Holy Spirit said that Barnabas and Paul were to be set apart for a work. Read Ephesians 3:8 in the margin. To what work was Paul called?

While the apostle Peter was called to preach to the Jews (Gal. 2:7), Paul was the apostle to the Gentiles. It wasn't that he didn't preach to the Hebrew people. After all, when he entered a new city, it was his custom to go first to the synagogue to preach. But with the Jews' rejection, Paul would then move on to the Gentiles. And most of Paul's missionary journeys were to Gentile lands.

> ✣ **Read once again what Paul penned in Ephesians 2:10. This was for the Ephesian believers, but it is also for you. Change the verse into the first person and write it below.**

Just as Paul had been called to the work of preaching to the Gentiles and Peter was called to preach to the Jews, God has prepared good works in advance for you to do as well. Is that hard for you to believe? Sometimes it is easy to glamorize biblical characters. But remember, they were ordinary people with an extraordinary God. Before the foundation of the world, you were chosen (Eph. 1:4), and works were prepared for you in Christ Jesus to do during your time here on this earth.

> ✣ **Do you have trouble believing that God has works planned for you? Why or why not?**

"God delights to do impossible things through improbable people to impart exceeding grace to undeserving recipients."

—Chip Ingram[94]

> ✣ **What do you think the works God has planned for you involve? Take a moment to also reflect what they might have been in the past.**

If you were with me for the *Greater Glory* Bible study, we traced the glory of God through the Scriptures and we discovered that in Christ, you are one of the ways the glory of God is revealed. *You* are to be an instrument of His glory in all you do. And just as the Lord had plans for the disciples, the Lord has good plans for you. It doesn't mean things will always be easy. Paul went through many trials and hardships as he fulfilled the call on his life, which we will see tomorrow. But because the Lord was in the journey, it was still good. It was filled with purpose, and it brought glory to God.

What is the Lord laying on your heart? Where are your passions? What injustice bothers you? Perhaps He is birthing a work in you now. Maybe it is to be the best parent to your children as you lead and direct them in the ways of the Lord. Maybe it is to serve in your church or be a light in your workplace. Maybe God is birthing a radical love for your neighbors. Maybe it is to champion a cause dear to the heart of God or share the love of Jesus through art, writing, or music. What kinds of things burden your heart? What does your heart long to see? The possibilities are endless, not because of you and your abilities, but because of the God we serve.

Read what Paul says in 1 Corinthians 2:9. What do you think about this verse?

Have you put God in a box? It can be easy to unknowingly dictate what we think He is capable of, and our minds tend to minimize what is possible. We think in the natural, but God operates in the supernatural. Our minds may not have even conceived what the Lord has prepared for us who love Him. God is bigger than you think. He is more detailed than you know, and He can do more than you imagine.

Once Paul encountered Jesus, there was no going back. He was full force on a mission to reach the lost Gentiles. That was the task appointed to him. To what is God calling you? Think, pray, and dream big. Stay close to the Lord, and submit to His will. Set your heart for journey and the open road of possibilities, and you will witness marvelous acts of God's love, kindness, might, and power. God can do the extraordinary with a willing heart!

"Now to him who is able to do immeasurably more than all we ask or imagine, according to his power that is at work within us, to him be glory in the church and in Christ Jesus throughout all generations, for ever and ever! Amen." Ephesians 3:20–21

> A heart for journey has faith that God can do the extraordinary through ordinary people.

Day Four

Yesterday, we saw how Paul was called to preach to the Gentiles. That is the work God appointed for him to do. Have you given any more thought to what works God has called you? If you're not sure, keep an eye open because the Lord may just start birthing a desire in your heart that will serve His purpose in your life—something that will bring joy to you and great glory to His name.

Let's take a look at what Paul is up to now in the book of Acts. I can tell you that Paul and Barnabas continued to preach and teach about Jesus at continued risk to their own lives. Often times, as we pursue the call of God on our lives, we will face hardship and opposition. Think back to Ezra and Nehemiah, whom we looked at in week 2. Following God isn't always a walk in the park. The enemy will work to stop anything that brings glory to Jesus. So what do we do in those situations? Let's see what Paul did in today's lesson.

Are you up for facing a little opposition with Paul? Record what happened to Paul as revealed in the following verses.

In Damascus, Acts 9:22–23

In Jerusalem, Acts 9:28–30

In Pisidian Antioch, Acts 13:44–45, 50

In Iconium, Acts 14:3–7

In Lystra, Acts 14:19–20

What did Paul do after he was dragged out of the city?

In Thyatira, Acts 16:22–24

In Corinth, Acts 18:5–6

In Jerusalem, Acts 21:30–36, Acts 23:12

In Caesarea, Acts 24:23, 27

✣ **And as if that wasn't enough, read 2 Corinthians 11:22–28. What else did Paul go through?**

> *"And now, compelled by the Spirit, I am going to Jerusalem, not knowing what will happen to me there. I only know that in every city the Holy Spirit warns me that prison and hardships are facing me. However, I consider my life worth nothing to me; my only aim is to finish the race and complete the task the Lord Jesus has given me—the task of testifying to the good news of God's grace."*
>
> —ACTS 20:22–24

Glance back at everything Paul faced. What makes someone keep going after such trouble? City after city, Paul endured persecution and yet, he persevered. He even entered into situations knowing in advance that he would face hardships. See Acts 20:22–24 in the margin.

Why did Paul persevere through it all? I'd like to suggest the following ideas.

Paul not only knew who Jesus was, but he also *knew Him* personally. He encountered the risen Jesus on that road to Damascus, and it was something that was never going to leave him. He knew Jesus was alive and real. Paul even shared that what he knew was revealed by Jesus Himself (Gal. 1:12). There was relationship there.

Paul knew God was with him and that He was in control. In Acts 18:9–11 while Paul was in Corinth, the Lord spoke to him in a vision and said, "Do not be afraid; keep on speaking, do not be silent. For I am with you, and no one is going to attack and harm you, because I have many people in this city." Paul did not lack confidence in the reality of God's presence as well as His sovereignty in all situations.

Paul knew that nothing could separate him from God. In Romans 8:38–39, Paul wrote, "For I am convinced that neither death nor life, neither angels nor demons, neither the present nor the future, nor any powers, neither height nor depth, nor anything else in all creation, will be able to separate us from the love of God that is in Christ Jesus our Lord." Paul had the full assurance of God's unfailing love.

Paul knew the will of God and willingly submitted to it. When God called Paul to go to Macedonia, he did (Acts 16:6–10). When leaving Ephesus, Paul promised that he would come back if it was God's will (Acts 18:21). The trust he had for where the Lord wanted him and would direct him allowed for a deep confidence in stepping out of comfort and into potential trouble. Paul was an instrument, and he knew God's will would prevail.

Paul had hope for the future. He believed that to be absent from the body was to be present with the Lord (2 Cor. 5:8). Whatever was done to his physical body wasn't eternal. He saw the big picture of life after death and knew that anything that happened in his earthly life was a blip on the radar when compared to an eternity with the Lord. He lived in light of eternity.

❖ **Which of these things could help you persevere? How?**

Let's close the day by reading a passage from Paul's hand. Please read 2 Corinthians 4:7–9. How did this play out in Paul's life?

When I was in college, my friend Tara and I took a pottery class. Oh how we loved it! We made all kinds of things. One of my favorite pieces currently sits in my office china cabinet. It is a light brown bowl with the rim pressed down on opposite sides. After I made it on the wheel, I had taken my fingers and pushed the lip of the bowl down. I didn't destroy it, nor did I crush it. I just pressed it. Why? To remind me of this verse. And even though the bowl was pressed and dented, it is still serving a purpose today.

On our journeys, we will feel pressed. We will experience hard times on the road of faith, but like Paul can we say that we are not crushed nor destroyed? No matter our current condition, we can still be used by God. The treasure of the jar is to show that all-surpassing power is from God and not from us. We can't do this by ourselves. We lack the power and the might. But God does not. He is able. Oh yes, He is able.

Keep on keeping on, my friend. You've got this!

A heart for journey perseveres.

Day Five

Today, I am having my refrigerator repaired for the fifth time in seven years. I told Dan we probably should start looking for a new one, but for the meantime, repairs are in order. Each time, the issue has started with a little, buzzing noise. It is a background hum and not too bad. But shortly thereafter, it becomes the most annoying, loud, buzzing sound of all—one that can be heard from the basement to the second floor of our house. And my friend, it makes me feel like I'm going crazy. Our kitchen is central to family life, but when the dissonance is at full volume, I can't take being in there for long. Despite the number of times we have emptied and thawed the fridge in an attempt to fix it on our own, it always ends with a service call.

The last time it started, I called for service immediately to get on the schedule. After I made the call and scheduled the appointment, I realized the buzzing didn't really bother me. It was so weird. The volume hadn't changed. The annoying tone hadn't diminished. It was me. I realized I was handling it better because I knew the end was in sight. I knew the solution was in front of me. I knew that the victory over the noise was coming.

And it dawned on me how this is true for life as well. When we can keep the end picture in our mind (the end being the glorious future we have in store with Jesus), does that help us handle the bumps and bruises along the road now? Yes, I think it does.

Being able to keep our eyes on the victory can change our mindset and the way we live our lives. It gives hope of something different than what we're facing currently or what we see in the world. It puts the end in view and our eyes on the horizon. So let's get a little taste of our future today. Turn to Isaiah 35, and let's search for the final highway.

Read Isaiah 35:1–2. What is being described in the first two verses?

If we were to we read this chapter in context with the bleakness and desolation found in Isaiah 34, the 35th chapter of Isaiah would be a breath of fresh air. Scholars differ on whether this chapter is referring to the return of the exiles, the millennial rule of Christ, the new heaven and earth, or all of them.[95] And that's okay. I tend to think it is a figurative description of our future when all is set right in the world, Jesus is on the throne, and restoration is at hand.

Isaiah 35 is a picture of those who have trusted in the Lord, now coming home on what was a highway in the desert but is now transformed into a beautiful garden.[96] Did you notice how the wilderness is rejoicing? The desert is in bloom!

Each morning before school, the kids and I watch *World Watch*, a 10-minute news program with a biblical worldview. It is like the old style news programs, presented without political bias. I love that it keeps us up to date with current events and also exposes us to feature stories from around the globe. Each episode ends with the same, exact phrase, "And remember, whatever the news, the purpose of the Lord will stand." How cool is that? It's a great reminder to keep everything in perspective and see the big picture as we process what is going on in the world today. God's purpose *will* prevail. His victory is sure. How would your day sound different if you reminded yourself of that each evening?

> "And remember, whatever the news, the purpose of the Lord will stand."
>
> —WORLD WATCH

Last week, one of the stories was about Chile's Atacama Desert. The Atacama Desert is usually one of the most desolate and barren places in the world, receiving only about half an inch of rain annually. But every three to five years, after a heavy rainfall in the southern region of Atacama, the desert blooms with vibrant and beautiful flowers. The rain causes seeds that were lying dormant in the ground to germinate. This year with such a stunning display, the President of Chile is proposing that the area be made into a national park called Desierto Florido which means flowering desert.[97]

What a sight to see a desert in bloom! When I think of how, since the fall of man, creation has been groaning for restoration (Romans 8:19–22), how lovely it will be to see the complete renewal and restoration of the whole earth. The glory of Lebanon and the splendor of Carmel and Sharon will be given to the desert (Isa. 35:2). The glory of Lebanon was found in its marvelous cedars, and Carmel and Sharon boasted all sorts of trees and plant life.[98] The dry desert is being given life. And what does the life of the desert reveal? Travelers will see the glory and splendor of the Lord Almighty.

Just as we saw in Psalm 84 where we first started in week 1, the desert is transformed. It is teeming with springs, with life, and with beauty. It has been a long time since I visited a desert. I remember seeing a little plant here and there, but by no means was it lush. The contrast would be stunning!

In the next verses, Isaiah bolstered the travelers with encouraging words. What encouragement do you see in Isaiah 35:3–4? Circle the one that encourages you most right now.

I love the protective image of the Father in these verses. What comfort a child receives when she knows her parents will do everything to protect and save her. That is our Heavenly Father, only He has the capability to do so, every single time. Your Father in Heaven is strong and mighty. Your God will come and show up on your behalf.

Read verses 5–7. What is the overall theme pictured here?

What we see is wholeness and restoration: the eyes of the blind opened, the ears of the deaf unstopped, the lame leaping about, and the mute shouting for joy. I know people who long for wholeness in their bodies and in the bodies of their loved ones. What a joyous day that will be!

Read these words penned by Thomas Moore:

> Come ye disconsolate, where 'er ye languish;
> Come to the mercy-seat, fervently kneel;
> Here bring your wounded hearts, here tell your anguish;
> Earth has no sorrow that Heaven cannot heal.[99]

✢ **Oh yes, there will be a day when all will be set right. Turn to Revelation 21:3–7. What is the outcome for the children of God?**

✢ **Knowing *that* is in our future, how does that make you feel?**

Turn back to Isaiah 35 and read verses 8–10. What is the highway called and who is it for?

At last, we see the glorious highway to Zion. Whether the literal city of Jerusalem or the future hope we possess in Christ, our destination is the place of God's dwelling. This is our final highway—one that has been prepared for us. And it is for those who walk in the Way. Does that cause you to think back to our lesson in Acts from the other day and the early Christians being called followers of the Way?

This highway is called the Way of Holiness, but let's remember we have not earned this right to tread here. This path is for those who stand in the holiness of Jesus. With our sinful nature, we are not eligible on our own. But when we stand justified in Jesus, then we can enter. (Justified is a legal term that means we are not pronounced guilty. We are declared righteous in God's sight because the innocence of Jesus has covered us.)

We are the redeemed who will walk this path. And how will we walk it? Isaiah 35:10 says, "and those the LORD has rescued will return. They will enter Zion with singing; everlasting joy will crown their heads. Gladness and joy will overtake them and sorrow and sighing will flee away." This last verse is echoed almost verbatim in Isaiah 51:11. Can you imagine being overtaken with a gladness and joy that doesn't end? I love watching clips of videos with little children laughing uncontrollably, amused sometimes by the simplest thing. Ah, joy—everlasting joy—is our future!

> ✻**Turn with me one last time to Psalm 84:5. Read the words slowly, taking each one in. Has your perspective on journey changed these last five weeks?**

Our journeys will have ups and downs, twists and turns, mountains and valleys. But as we journey with God, we will find purpose, strength, passion, perspective, truth, community, fulfillment, and joy. The journey is still good because of Him. *Our God* is wonderful and He is faithful. There will come a day when we draw our last breath and then, in an instant, faith will become sight. And we will see Him as He is. I can't wait!

It's a great adventure with a glorious destination. But for now, *will you have a heart for journey?*

I can't wait to share the final video lesson with you. There is one more sweet thing you'll enjoy on your journey.

"So is my word that goes out from my mouth: It will not return to me empty, but will accomplish what I desire and achieve the purpose for which I sent it. You will go out in joy and be led forth in peace; the mountains and hills will burst into song before you, and all the trees of the field will clap their hands. Instead of the thornbush will grow the juniper and instead of briers the myrtle will grow. This will be for the LORD's renown, for an everlasting sign, that will endure forever." Isaiah 55:11–13

> A heart for journey sees the open road and knows that full restoration awaits. One day our faith will be made sight.

WATCH THE WEEK 5 VIDEO

A Song of Praise on our Lips

Scriptures in this Session: Psalm 126:1–3, Psalm 40:1–3

Also mentioned: Psalm 137, 1 Corinthians 2:9, Psalm 121:3–8

The pilgrim's song _____ _____ who God is and what He has done.

The pilgrim's song reveals a _____.

The nature of the song is a hymn of _____.

The pilgrim's song of praise gives Jesus the _____ _____ in our lives—on the throne.

Video lessons are available at KristenTiber.com/AHeartForJourneyVideos.

ABOUT THE AUTHOR

Kristen Tiber

Kristen is an author, speaker, and women's Bible study teacher. She is married to Dan and homeschools their two teens, Peter and Anna. Kristen and her husband have the joy of teaching the high school Sunday School class each week at their church. As much as Kristen absolutely loves teaching the Bible, she equally loves being a student of God's Word. Her desire is to see the Scriptures come alive for others as she encourages women to live faithful, impactful lives, and ultimately lift up the name of Jesus and glorify Him. Her books include *Greater Glory*, *At the Well*, and *Teach Me to Serve*. Kristen can be found at KristenTiber.com, where she inspires others to live with purpose in all seasons of life.

WOULD YOU LIKE FIVE PRINTABLE SCRIPTURE MEMORY VERSES TO ENCOURAGE YOU ON YOUR JOURNEY WITH GOD?

Visit the video page for *A Heart for Journey*
and scroll to the bottom to download the free printables.

WERE YOU BLESSED BY THIS BIBLE STUDY?

*Please consider leaving a review on Amazon or Goodreads
to help encourage others with message of this study.*

Another Bible Study From Kristen

Greater Glory

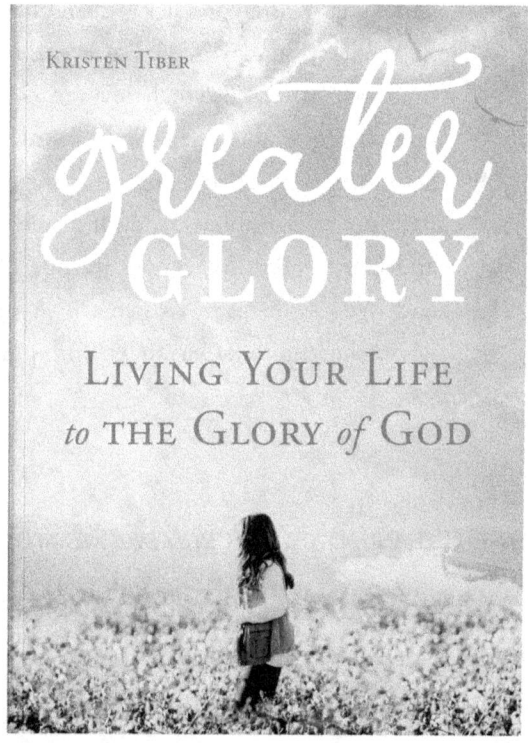

Can *you* bring God glory? Absolutely! You can bring glory to God in the things you do, the way you live, the words you speak, and the thoughts you think.

Join Kristen in a study of the glory of God as she traces His glory chronologically through the Scriptures starting with creation. You will discover how *you* can bring God greater glory through your obedience, your patience, the desires of your heart, and even your suffering.

How to Have a Personal Relationship with Jesus

You may have heard people talk about having a personal relationship with God, and maybe that has left you with some questions. *Can I really know God? Does He know me? What does it mean to have a personal relationship when I can't see the One I'm supposed to be getting to know? How do you know if you're in a relationship with God? And what difference does it even make?*

Well first, let's take a couple of steps back. We'll start with what we see in nature. In the Bible, we are told that creation reveals the glory of God. Creation also points to the fact that there *is* a Creator. When we look out our window and see the beauty, the design, the detail, and complexity of all of creation, we see the evidence of a masterful Creator. All of this did not come from nothing. Someone had to create it. Just like this book didn't pop into existence, but rather someone wrote it, someone printed it, and someone made sure it got to you—the same is true with creation. The complex design of the human body alone points us to the reality of forethought and a meticulous Designer.

So in order to talk about relationship, we have to first acknowledge that there is a God. In the Bible (the inspired and authoritative Word of God given to us), we learn about Him. We learn about His character, His deeds, His holiness, and His love for us.

But there is a problem.

You see, we (you and I) have a sin problem. We do sinful things. We think unholy thoughts. We can be selfish and prideful. And in all this, we sin against our Creator. Because God is perfectly holy and just, there are consequences for doing wrong, and we must face judgment for our actions. Think about if someone in your family was horribly injured by a thief who entered your home. The thief was arrested and appeared in court before a judge. What would you think of the judge if he just released the thief and did not punish the crime? You would think he was a bad judge, right? A good and righteous judge delivers consequences for sin. God must do the same.

And while you may think you are basically a good person, I am guessing that all your thoughts haven't always been perfect, kind, good, and holy. We have a problem because of our sin. The

Bible says that all have sinned and fallen short of the glory of God (Romans 3:23) and that the wages of sin is death (Romans 6:23). Because of our sin against a holy God, we deserve death and an eternity separated from Him.

Now, you may be thinking right now that no one can be perfect. And you are correct! None of us are righteous enough to earn our way into Heaven. Therefore, we are without any possible hope if left to our own devices. But that is where God, in His love for us, stepped in to provide a solution.

John 3:16–17 tells us, "For God so loved the world that he gave his one and only Son, that whoever believes in him shall not perish but have eternal life. For God did not send his Son into the world to condemn the world, but to save the world through him."

God sent Jesus to pay the price of our sin. Jesus lived a perfect life. He was without sin and therefore, was a worthy party to make payment. But the payment was something so horrible, that many times people have a hard time believing that someone would do this for them. Jesus allowed himself to be crucified on a cross, facing an excruciating death, and in doing so, He took the punishment that should have been ours—death. Our sin was paid for by the blood of Jesus.

But equally amazing is that Jesus didn't stay dead. On the third day after His crucifixion, He rose from the dead. And the evidence for the actual and physical resurrection of Christ is astounding. (Take a look at the *Case for Christ* by Lee Strobel).[100] The Son of God rose from the dead and was seen by over 500 witnesses, in 12 different locations, over 40 days.

You see, Christians believe not only that Jesus died in their place and paid the penalty of their sin, but they also believe that He rose from the dead and that they will spend all of eternity with Him. That is the future for which Christians rely upon, based on the authority of God's Word.

Though where we spend all of eternity following our earthly existence is paramount, the start of your relationship with God begins here on earth. Becoming a Christian means recognizing that you are in need of a Savior. It means not only believing and confessing that Jesus is your Savior, that He saved you from the penalty of sin (an eternity away from Him), but also submitting to Him as Lord of your life. There is a surrender that takes place. And while that may sound like a lot to swallow, keep in mind you are yielding your life to the One who set aside His glory to come to earth, to die in your place. He sacrificed Himself freely for you because He loves you! Isn't that amazing? The Creator of the whole world loves YOU!

And there is nothing you can do to earn that love. Jesus' sacrificial death on the cross is a free gift. We stand innocent before the Righteous Judge not because of what we have done, but because of what His Son did for us. We are found "not guilty" because of the blood Jesus shed on our behalf.

Scripture tells us that once we believe in Jesus, His Holy Spirit comes and dwells within us. He is alive in us. Sure we will still sin, but as we learn and grow, our desire is to be more like Jesus. And once you have entered into this relationship with God, you are His child. "Yet to all who did receive him, to those who believed in his name, he gave the right to become children of God" (John 1:12). As His child, you have full access to Him, and He delights in you.

If you are feeling the need for a Savior, if you want to receive Jesus into your life, tell Him now. And once you do that, I encourage you to tell someone else. Tell a friend. Tell your pastor. If you are not in a Bible-teaching, Bible-believing church, find one. It is of great importance to be connected to a local body of believers. They will help you grow, and they will challenge, encourage, and equip you. Meanwhile, I am so glad you are in this study. There may be many new concepts and ideas, but hang in there. Following Jesus will be the absolute best adventure of your life!

Leader's Guide

Thank you so much for leading a small group through *A Heart for Journey*! I am praying that the Lord directs you as you lead your group each week. Your responsibilities will include facilitating discussion time, leading in prayer, selecting worship songs (if applicable), and making preparations for the group to watch the online teaching video each week.

While the teaching video is integral to the study, please know that the small group aspect of your time together is such a valuable component as well. This time will allow for your group to grow and bond together, and get to know each other on a deeper level. How I love women's small groups! Thoughts and feelings are shared. Faith is built. Fellowship is increased. Encouragement is given. This is a wonderful opportunity to grow and learn from each other.

This study consists of five weeks of work in the book and six online teaching videos—an introduction video and a video following each week in the workbook. This means you will meet six times as a group.

Introduction Week

Please feel free to change up the order of activities below to best suit your group.

Welcome your group and distribute workbooks. If you have women who do not know each other, names tags can be very helpful for the first few weeks.

Share prayer requests and open in prayer: Provide time each week for ladies to share prayer requests, and then lift the requests up to the Lord. Remind the group of the need for confidentiality on things that should not be shared beyond the group.

Depending on the size of your group, invite the ladies to go around the circle and pray. There is no pressure to pray; no one has to pray aloud if they would rather not. You, as the leader, should be the last one to pray and as you close, make sure to pray for any requests not already lifted up.

Encourage the ladies to write down the requests in their books and pray about them during the week.

A Heart for Journey

Watch the introduction video: All videos can be accessed through www.KristenTiber.com/AHeartForJourneyVideos. An email address is required to view the lessons. Video lengths are listed on the video library page. All videos *except* the introduction video have an accompanying study guide to be filled out in the workbook.

Discussion: The first week you meet is the Introduction, and there is no homework to be discussed. You can use the questions below for this first day.

1. Introduce yourself and share your favorite vacation spot.

2. Are you more destination or journey-minded?

3. What do you think it means to have a heart set on pilgrimage?

4. Do you think our culture tends toward destination or journey? And why?

5. Why do you think the Lord is interested in the journey?

6. What kinds of things detract from a journeying mindset?

7. What do you want out of this study?

Worship: If possible, spend time together in worship. Song suggestions are listed on the same webpage as the videos.

Close in prayer.

All Other Weeks

Share prayer requests and open in prayer.

Discussion: Discuss answers from the workbook questions indicated by ✻. There are usually 2–3 questions per day. You will not be discussing every question for the entire week. Do share your own answers and contribute to the conversation as well, but try to let others answer first.

A Heart for Journey

Allow for any other thoughts or comments about what was studied during the week. Usually, someone will have something they would like to bring up, a thought they would like to share, or a question they would like to ask, etc. Be aware of your time, however, if you are on a schedule.

Keep your group on task. As you most likely already know, group discussion can easily tangent off to different topics. Try your best to redirect your group to the discussion at hand. But also know, if there is a pressing need, feel free to take the time to address it accordingly!

Watch the online video.

>Week One: Road Ready

>Week Two: A Return Trip

>Week Three: Together

>Week Four: A Heart to Serve

>Week Five: The Road Ahead

Worship. Song suggestions are listed on the same webpage as the videos.

Close in prayer.

Acknowledgements

To my family: Dan, Peter, Anna, and my mom, Beth. Your support always amazes me. Thank you for reading, helping, supporting, and cheerleading.

To the ladies at my church who went through this study as I taught it the first time. You put up with typos in the text and the adjustments we made to accommodate so many women, but your hearts were for the journey. What a blessing it is for me to be in community with you all, and I am so grateful for your encouragement in this study. I praise God for how He worked through our time in Bible study together!

Oh Tara! The Lord certainly blessed me with a friend like you—who lets me bounce every thought and run every idea by you, who analyzes and edits with a fine eye and loves the English language (unlike me). We have known each other for more than half of our lives, and I'm so thankful for you!

Melinda, you are amazingly talented, and I enjoyed working with you so much. Knowing that the book was in your very capable hands from cover design to formatting eased my mind and made the process so much easier. I look forward to working with you again and again.

To the ladies who attended the filming sessions, thank you for all your kindness and support (and patience with power outages). Your presence was such a blessing, and I appreciate you all so much!

Raquel, you were an answer to prayer. Your heart for serving the Lord has been a great blessing to me. Thank you for using your skills and talents in ministry!

A very special thank you to Riverview Church for graciously hosting our filming sessions. I can't tell you how much I appreciate your hospitality and heart for Kingdom work!

Chris, you were the piece of the puzzle I didn't expect, but the Lord knew beforehand. Your kindness and heart for helping has been such a blessing. I don't know anyone with a greater personal desire to serve the Lord so generously with his or her time and valuable skills than you. Thank you!

Works Cited

1 D.A. Carson, ed., *NIV Biblical Theology Study Bible* (Grand Rapids: Zondervan, 2018), 924.

2 *Cambridge Bible for Schools and Colleges,* "Psalm 84," Bible Hub (website), accessed June 23, 2022, https://biblehub.com/commentaries/cambridge/psalms/84.htm.

3 Carson, *NIV Biblical*, 961.

4 Ronald F. Youngblood, ed., "Rehoboam." *Nelson's New Illustrated Bible Dictionary* (Nashville: Thomas Nelson Publishers, 1995), 1075.

5 Youngblood, "Amos." *Nelson's,* 51.

6 Youngblood, "Bethel." *Nelson's,* 180.

7 *Strong's Concordance,* "esher," Bible Hub (website), accessed June 24, 2022, https://biblehub.com/hebrew/835.htm.

8 *Strong's Concordance,* "mesillah," Bible Hub (website), accessed June 24, 2022, https://biblehub.com/hebrew/4546.htm.

9 *Cambridge Online.*

10 Charles J. Ellicott, *Ellicott's Commentary on the Whole Bible*, vol. 4 (Grand Rapids: Zondervan, 1954), 213.

11 Willem A. VanGemeren and Frank E. Gaebelein, eds., *The Expositor's Bible Commentary,* vol. 5 (Grand Rapids: Zondervan, 1991), 544.

12 Albert Barnes, *Barnes' Notes: Psalms* (Grand Rapids: Baker Books, 2005), 342.

13 *Cambridge Online.*

14 Carson, *NIV Biblical*, 977.

15 Warren W. Wiersbe, *The Bible Exposition Commentary: Old Testament Wisdom and Poetry* (Colorado Springs: Cook Communications Ministries, 2003), 245.

16 Wiersbe, *Bible Exposition: Old Testament Wisdom and Poetry,* 245.

17 Warren W. Wiersbe, *The Bible Exposition Commentary: Old Testament History* (Colorado Springs: Cook Communications Ministries, 2004), 604.

18 Wiersbe, *Bible Exposition: Old Testament History,* 604,606.

19　Frank E. Gaebelein and Edwin Yamauchi, eds., *The Expositor's Bible Commentary,* vol. 4 (Grand Rapids: Zondervan, 1988), 650.

20　Wiersbe, *Bible Exposition: Old Testament History, 619.*

21　Gaebelein and Yamauchi, *Expositor's,* vol. 4, 650.

22　Wiersbe, *Bible Exposition: Old Testament History, 619.*

23　Carson, *NIV Biblical,* 758.

24　Chip Ingram, "Holy Ambition - Create A Strategic Plan, Part 1." accessed May 11, 2022, in *Living on the Edge,* podcast, MP3 audio, https://livingontheedge.org/product/holy-ambition-mp3.

25　Jerry A. Pattengale, Ph.D. ed., *Genesis to Ruth* (USA: Museum of the Bible, 2016), 81.

26　Youngblood, "God, Names of – Jehovah-jireh." *Nelson's,* 503.

27　Spiros Zodhiates, Th.D., ex ed., "8011: ra'ah l." *Hebrew-Greek Key Word Study Bible* (Chattanooga: AMG Publishers, 1996), 2010.

28　Zodhiates, *Hebrew-Greek,* 1549.

29　Linda Smallwood, "The God Behind the Names," My Redeemer Lives (blog) accessed September 3, 2022, http://www.myredeemerlives.com/namesofgod/namesofgod.html.

30　Stone, Nathan*, Names of God* (Chicago: Moody Press, 2010), 79–80.

31　Carson, *NIV Biblical,* 760.

32　Wiersbe, *Bible Exposition: Old Testament History,* 622.

33　Mark Dever, Senior Pastor, Capitol Hill Baptist Church, Washington D.C.

34　*Pulpit Commentary,* "Ecclesiastes 4," Bible Hub (website), accessed September 16, 2022, https://biblehub.com/commentaries/pulpit/ecclesiastes/4.htm.

35　Mark 9:2, Luke 8:51, Matthew 26:37

36　Dr. James Merritt, "Better Together," *Touching Lives with Dr. James Merritt* (website), accessed September 20, 2022, https://www.touchinglives.org/devotionals/better-together.

37　Wiersbe, *Bible Exposition: Old Testament History,* 179.

38　J. Vernon McGee, *Thru The Bible,* vol. 2 (Nashville: Thomas Nelson Publishers, 1982), 90.

39　Daniel I. Block, *The New American Commentary, Judges-Ruth* (Nashville: Broadman & Holman Publishers, 1999), 638.

40　Wiersbe, *Bible Exposition: Old Testament History,* 182.

41　McGee, *Thru,* vol. 2, 298

42 Carson, *NIV Biblical*, 432.

43 F.B. Huey Jr. and Frank E. Gaebelein, eds., *The Expositor's Bible Commentary*, vol. 3 (Grand Rapids: Zondervan, 1992), 533.

44 Block, *New American*, 725.

45 Block, *New American*, 729

46 Wiersbe, *Bible Exposition: Old Testament History*, 198.

47 "What does the Bible say about togetherness?" *Got Questions (website)*, accessed September 26, 2022, https://www.gotquestions.org/Bible-togetherness.html.

48 F.C. Cook, *Barnes' Notes: Exodus to Esther* (Grand Rapids: Baker Books, 2005), 56.

49 Simon J. Kistemaker, *New Testament Commentary: Acts* (Grand Rapids, Baker Academic, 1990), 111.

50 Susan Hunt, *Spiritual Mothering* (Wheaton: Crossway, 1992), 82.

51 Hunt, *Spiritual*, 84.

52 Hunt, *Spiritual*, 69.

53 Hunt, *Spiritual*, 75.

54 Youngblood, "Jonah, Book Of." *Nelson's*, 698.

55 Youngblood, "Jonah, Book Of." *Nelson's*, 698.

56 Carson, *NIV Biblical*, 1582.

57 John H. Walton, Victor H. Matthews, and Mark W. Chavalas, *The IVP Bible Background Commentary* (Downers Grove, IL: InterVarsity Press, 2000), 777.

58 Warren W. Wiersbe, *The Bible Exposition Commentary: Old Testament Prophets* (Colorado Springs: Cook Communications Ministries, 2002), 383.

59 Wiersbe, *Bible Exposition: Old Testament Prophets*, 383

60 J. Vernon McGee, *Thru The Bible*, vol. 3 (Nashville: Thomas Nelson Publishers, 1982), 742.

61 *The Complete Jewish Study Bible* (Peabody, MA: Hendrickson Publishing Marketing, 2016), 833.

62 Walton, Matthews, and Chavalas, *IVP*, 777.

63 Walton, Matthews, and Chavalas, *IVP*, 777–778.

64 Wiersbe, *Bible Exposition: Old Testament Prophets*, 378.

65 Wiersbe, *Bible Exposition: Old Testament Prophets*, 379.

66 Youngblood, "Jonah, Book Of." *Nelson's*, 698.

67 McGee, *Thru*, vol. 3, 737.

68 Wiersbe, *Bible Exposition: Old Testament Prophets*, 382.

69 McGee, *Thru*, vol. 3, 752, 760.

70 McGee, *Thru*, vol. 3, 760.

71 Walton, Matthews, and Chavalas, *IVP*, 779.

72 McGee, *Thru*, vol. 3, 760.

73 McGee, *Thru*, vol. 3, 740.

74 Wiersbe, *Bible Exposition: Old Testament Prophets*, 385.

75 *Complete Jewish*, 162.

76 Menachem Posner, "Why do we read the Book of Jonah on Yom Kippur," *Chabad.org. (website)*, accessed October 3, 2022, https://www.chabad.org/library/article_cdo/aid/568512/jewish/Why-do-we-read-the-Book-of-Jonah-on-Yom-Kippur.htm.

77 *Complete Jewish*, 162.

78 Beth Moore, "Jonah: Angry Enough to Die, Part One." May 30, 2022, in *Living Proof Ministries* (podcast), https://subsplash.com/livingproofwithbethmoore/messages/mi/+mmfzkrn

79 H.L. Ellison and Frank E. Gaebelein, eds., *The Expositor's Bible Commentary*, vol. 7 (Grand Rapids: Zondervan, 1985), 385.

80 Rosaria Butterfield, *The Gospel Comes with a House Key* (audiobook), performed by Rosaria Butterfield, (ChristianAudio.com, 2018).

81 *Pulpit Commentary*, "Joshua 1," Bible Hub (website), accessed October 11, 2022, https://biblehub.com/commentaries/pulpit/joshua/1.htm.

82 Carson, *NIV Biblical*, 350.

83 Warren W. Wiersbe, *The Bible Exposition Commentary: New Testament* (Colorado Springs: Cook Communications Ministries, 2001), 52.

84 Wiersbe, *Bible Exposition: Old Testament Prophets*, 383.

85 VanGemeren and Gaebelein, *Expositor's*, vol. 5, 768.

86 McGee, *Thru*, vol. 2, 851.

87 McGee, *Thru*, vol. 2, 851.

88 VanGemeren and Gaebelein, *Expositor's*, vol. 5, 769.

89 VanGemeren and Gaebelein, *Expositor's,* vol. 5, 772.

90 *Acts; Life Change Series* (Colorado Springs: NavPress, 1990), 95.

91 *Strong's Concordance*, "hodos," Bible Hub (website), accessed October 17, 2022, https://biblehub.com/greek/3598.htm.

92 *Acts,* 96.

93 Greg Lanier, "No, 'Saul the Persecutor; Did Not Become 'Paul the Apostle,'" *The Gospel Coalition* (website), accessed October 17, 2022, https://www.thegospelcoalition.org/article/no-saul-the-persecutor-did-not-become-paul-the-apostle/.

94 Chip Ingram, "Good to Great: Dream Great Dreams, Part 1." accessed October 9, 2022, in *Living on the Edge,* podcast, app, *https://livingontheedge.org/broadcast/dream-great-dreams*.

95 Carson, *NIV Biblical,* 1225.

96 Carson, *NIV Biblical,* 1225.

97 Taylor Hebert, "Chile's Atacama Desert Flowers," *World Watch (video),* aired October 11, 2022, https://worldwatch.news.

98 Geoffrey W. Grogan and Frank E. Gaebelein, eds., *The Expositor's Bible Commentary,* Vol. 6. (Grand Rapids: Zondervan, 1986), 221.

99 Thomas Moore (1779–1852), "Come Ye Disconsolate." Altered by Thomas Hastings (1784–1872).

100 Lee Strobel, *The Case for Christ,* Updated & Expanded Edition (Grand Rapids: Zondervan, 2016).

www.ingramcontent.com/pod-product-compliance
Lightning Source LLC
Chambersburg PA
CBHW080931020526
44118CB00038B/2474